Palgrave Studies in Migration History

Series Editors
Philippe Rygiel
École normale supérieure de Lyon
Saint-Germain-du-Puy, France

Per-Olof Grönberg
Luleå University of Technology
Luleå, Sweden

David Feldman
Birkbeck College—University of London
London, UK

Marlou Schrover
Leiden University
Leiden, Zuid-Holland, The Netherlands

This series explores the history of migration, from antiquity to the present day and across a wide geographical scope. Taking a broad definition of migration, the editors welcome books that consider all forms of mobility, including cross-border mobility, internal migration and forced migration. These books investigate the causes and consequences of migration, whether for economic, religious, humanitarian or political reasons, and the policies and organizations that facilitate or challenge mobility. Considering responses to migration, the series looks to migrants' experiences, the communities left behind and the societies in which they settled. The editors welcome proposals for monographs, edited collections and Palgrave Pivots.

More information about this series at
http://www.palgrave.com/gp/series/15185

Francesca Falk

Gender Innovation and Migration in Switzerland

Francesca Falk
University of Fribourg
Fribourg, Switzerland

Published with the support of the Swiss National Science Foundation

Palgrave Studies in Migration History
ISBN 978-3-030-01625-8   ISBN 978-3-030-01626-5 (eBook)
https://doi.org/10.1007/978-3-030-01626-5

Library of Congress Control Number: 2018957067

© The Editor(s) (if applicable) and The Author(s) 2019. This book is an open access publication.

Open Access This book is licensed under the terms of the Creative Commons Attribution-NonCommercial-NoDerivatives 4.0 International License (http://creativecommons.org/licenses/by-nc-nd/4.0/), which permits any noncommercial use, sharing, distribution and reproduction in any medium or format, as long as you give appropriate credit to the original author(s) and the source, provide a link to the Creative Commons license and indicate if you modified the licensed material. You do not have permission under this license to share adapted material derived from this book or parts of it.

The images or other third party material in this book are included in the book's Creative Commons license, unless indicated otherwise in a credit line to the material. If material is not included in the book's Creative Commons license and your intended use is not permitted by statutory regulation or exceeds the permitted use, you will need to obtain permission directly from the copyright holder.

This work is subject to copyright. All commercial rights are reserved by the author(s), whether the whole or part of the material is concerned, specifically the rights of translation, reprinting, reuse of illustrations, recitation, broadcasting, reproduction on microfilms or in any other physical way, and transmission or information storage and retrieval, electronic adaptation, computer software, or by similar or dissimilar methodology now known or hereafter developed. Regarding these commercial rights a non-exclusive license has been granted to the publisher.

The use of general descriptive names, registered names, trademarks, service marks, etc. in this publication does not imply, even in the absence of a specific statement, that such names are exempt from the relevant protective laws and regulations and therefore free for general use.

The publisher, the authors, and the editors are safe to assume that the advice and information in this book are believed to be true and accurate at the date of publication. Neither the publisher nor the authors or the editors give a warranty, express or implied, with respect to the material contained herein or for any errors or omissions that may have been made. The publisher remains neutral with regard to jurisdictional claims in published maps and institutional affiliations.

Cover illustration: © Melisa Hasan

This Palgrave Pivot imprint is published by the registered company Springer Nature Switzerland AG
The registered company address is: Gewerbestrasse 11, 6330 Cham, Switzerland

For Anna and Vian—and for everyone who cared for them while I was working at the university

Acknowledgements

My special thanks for their help in drafting this book go to Cenk Akdoganbulut, Sarah Baumann, Simone Bleuer, Kijan Espahangizi, Marcel Falk, Hans Fässler, Donna Gabaccia, Hansjörg Höchner, Paola Höchner-Gallicani, Rohit Jain, Chad Jorgenson, Elisabeth Joris, Sherry Keith, Zoé Kergomard, Inés Mateos, Barbara Miller, Martin Mühlheim, Julia Nentwich, Patricia Purtschert, Linda Ratschiller, Bernhard C. Schär, Celeste Ugochukwu, Regina Wecker, Aglaia Wespe, and to my colleagues from *Studio Roma*. I would also like to thank two anonymous reviewers and the participants at the following events for their valuable questions and comments: 'From Colonisation to Globalisation', conference at the University of Bern (2018); 'Migration and Socio-Political Innovation', conference co-organised with *infoclio.ch* at the University of Fribourg (2018); the lecture at the *Casa d'Italia* invited by *Marche Mondiale des Femmes* (2018); the farewell event at the *Centro Italiano* in Appenzell (2018); the lecture at the University for Seniors in Schaffhausen (2018); the keynote at the Summer University of the Social Democratic Party of Switzerland in Chandolin (2017); the presentation at the 'Fribourg Forum for Contemporary History' at the University of Fribourg (2014 and 2018) and at the 'Colloquium in Contemporary and Eastern European History' at the University of Bern (2014). Finally, I would like to thank the staff of the *Swiss National Library*, the *University Library Bern*, the *Cantonal and University Library of Fribourg*, and the *State Archive of the Canton Bern*.

Contents

1 **Introduction**   1
Switzerland as a Straggler in Relation to Gender Equality   1
An Exploratory Interview   4
'As If I Had Made a Journey Back in Time'   5
Cooking and Sewing Courses for Girls, Geometry for Boys   7
Unequal Opportunities at School   10
Bring to the Fore Not Only Personal, But Also Structural Conditions   12

2 **Conceptual Clarifications**   15
Gender Innovation   15
The Intersection of Discrimination and Privileges and New Reconfigurations   16
A 'Migrantisation' of the Past   18
The Relationship Between Spatial and Social Change   20
Migration and Mobility   22
A Unified Analysis of Migration   23

3 **Changing Gendered Divisions of Work**   27
Nurses from Kerala   27
A Sedentary Bias in the History of Emigration   30
Colonial Constellations   33

4	**Nurseries**	39
	The First Nurseries	40
	The So-Called Boom Years	41
	There Is Never a Single Story	42
	Migration and the Development of Nurseries	46
	The Normalising Effect of an Infrastructure	49
	The Current Situation	51
	Male Staff Members with a so-Called Migrant Background	52
5	**Higher Education**	57
	Switzerland as a Pioneer—And What Lies Behind It	57
	The Oft-Omitted Impact of These 'Foreign' Students	59
	Feminist Forerunners Are not Unequivocal Heroines of History	60
	The First Female Full Professor in Switzerland—Born in the Russian Empire	61
	The First Extraordinara in Romandie—Born in the Russian Empire	64
	The First Extraordinara in German-Speaking Switzerland—Again Born in…	65
6	**Female Suffrage**	69
	Female Suffrage in Switzerland and Its Relation to Migration	70
	The First Formal Association Promoting Political and Legal Equality for Women	71
	Migrating Political Strategies	72
	The Last Stragglers	73
	An Indirect Experience of Migration	76
	Not Downplaying the Effects of Racism	77
	Women's Right to Vote in Cultural Memory	78
	Unseen Democratic Deficits in the Supposed Heartland of Democracy	80
	'A New Swiss Export Article: Instruction in Democracy'	81
	1929: Fighting Women in Nigeria and Switzerland	83
7	**Conclusion: An Awareness of Alternatives**	87
	Equal Rights Presented as Being Endangered by Migration	88
	Migration and the Creation of New Ideas and Practices	90
	Changing the Perspective Under Which Our Past Is Told and Our Future Imagined	92

CHAPTER 1

Introduction

Abstract This introduction shows how, from a 'migrant's perspective', the defects of a newly adopted home country become particularly visible. Such voices, while always individual, allow us to paint a picture of Switzerland's past that until now was seldom part of either Swiss historiography or collective memory. In this way, they bring to the fore not only private, but also structural conditions. And they make it possible to capture the political impact of everyday occurrences that are not passed down in other historical sources.

Keywords A 'migrant's perspective' · Switzerland as a straggler · Domestic education · Unequal opportunities at school

SWITZERLAND AS A STRAGGLER IN RELATION TO GENDER EQUALITY

In the boom years after the Second World War, Italians were by far the largest group of immigrants in Switzerland.[1] According to a common narrative in the history of migration, female 'migrants' coming

---

[1] There is extensive literature on Italian immigration to Switzerland. A compact overview is offered by Toni Ricciardi, *Breve storia dell'emigrazione italiana in Svizzera. Dall'esodo di massa alle nuove mobilità*, Roma: Donzelli editore 2018.

© The Author(s) 2019
F. Falk, *Gender Innovation and Migration in Switzerland*,
Palgrave Studies in Migration History,
https://doi.org/10.1007/978-3-030-01626-5_1

from the south discovered 'women's emancipation' through living in the supposedly more advanced north.[2] But Italian women coming to Switzerland also experienced the opposite. From a 'migrant's perspective', the defects of a newly adopted home country become particularly visible. Of course, Italian laws were not more progressive in every aspect. For instance, it was only in 1970 that divorce was introduced in Italy.[3] Nevertheless, some social and political rights for women—such as female suffrage, wage equality, or a family law involving equal duties and responsibilities—had been introduced years, in some cases even decades before this was the case in Switzerland.[4] For instance, gender equality before the law had been included in the Italian Constitution of 1948 as a result of Lina Merlin's work in the constituent assembly.[5] In Switzerland, it was only in 1981 that a similar article was added to the Constitution. Regarding maternity protection, women in Italy have benefited from job protection and financial compensation since the 1950s,[6] while in

[2] For such a perspective, see for example, Cristina Allemann-Ghionda, Conclusioni, in Allemann-Ghionda, Meyer-Sabino, and De Marchi Oechslin, *Donne italiane in Svizzera*, Basel: Dadò 1992, 269–288, 269. Andreina De Clementi, and Giovani e sole, *Il prezzo della ricostruzione. L'emigrazione italiana nel secondo dopoguerra*, Roma: Laterza 2010.

For a similar argument in regard to other groups see May B. Broda, East European Jewish Migration to Switzerland and the Formation of 'New Women', in Lewinsky and Mayoraz, *East European Jews in Switzerland*, Berlin and Boston: Walter de Gruyter 2013, 149–173.

[3] On the relative liberality of Swiss divorce law and its implementation in the canton of Bern at the beginning of the twentieth century, see Caroline Arni, *Entzweiungen. Die Krise der Ehe um 1900, Köln*, Wien and Weimar: Böhlau 2004.

[4] Sarah Baumann, *...und es kamen auch Frauen. Engagement italienischer Migrantinnen in Politik und Gesellschaft der Nachkriegsschweiz*, Zürich: Seismo 2014, 45; Claudia Kaufmann, Italien, *Die Stellung der Frau in der Schweiz. Teil IV: Frauenpolitik. Bericht der Eidgenössischen Kommission für Frauenfragen*, Bern: Eidgenössische Drucksachen und Materialzentrale 1984, 225–228.

[5] Claudia Galimberti, Un cuore pensante. Lina Merlin, in Cioni, Di Caro, Doni, Galimberti, Levi, Palieri, Sancin, Di San Marzano, Tagliaventi, and Valentini, *Donne della Repubblica*, Bologna: Società editrice il Mulino 2016, 113–128, 119.

[6] The law of 1971 'extended the maternity-leave provisions first introduced in the 1950s, granting women giving birth five months' leave at 80 percent of their salaries and the option of staying out for up to a year at 30 percent'. 'Modernization' and Welfare State Restructuring in Italy, in Michel and Mahon, *Child Care Policy at the Crossroads: Gender and Welfare State Restructuring*, Italy: The Impact on Child Care, New York: Routledge 2002, 171–190, 177.

Switzerland the legal implementation of compulsory maternity insurance with universal coverage failed in several federal referendums and therefore remained unrealised on the national level until 2005. In 1975, Italy instituted a family law that abolished the legal status of the man as head of the family, replacing it with the concept of the husband and wife as equal partners. In Switzerland, such a reform came into effect only in 1988. In the federal referendum on this law in 1985, more than half of Swiss men still rejected the reform, and the new law was only adopted thanks to the support of Swiss women.[7] According to the marriage law that remained in force until 1988, a married woman needed the consent of her husband if she wanted to work and the male head of the family had the right to choose where the family would live, even if such provisions were often no longer put into practice towards the end. Such unequal treatment also had an impact on children. For instance, if my mother had been Swiss and my father Italian, I would not have received Swiss citizenship when I was born in 1977.[8]

Already in 1967, such shortfalls were described by Maria Bonada in the newspaper *Emigrazione italiana*.[9] In Switzerland, this type of critique gained traction more broadly only with the rise of the new women's movement in the 1970s, as Sarah Baumann has shown in her inspiring book.[10]

---

[7] Elisabeth Joris and Heidi Witzig, *Frauengeschichte(n). Dokumente aus zwei Jahrhunderten zur Situation der Frauen in der Schweiz*, Zürich: Limmat Verlag 1991 (1986), 346.

[8] Die Stellung der Frau in der Schweiz. Teil III: Recht. Bericht der Eidgenössischen Kommission für Frauenfragen, Eidgenössische Drucksachen und Materialzentrale 1980, 5. Brigitte Studer, Citizenship as Contingent National Belonging: Married Women and Foreigners in Twentieth-Century Switzerland, *Gender & History* 13, 3 (2001), 622–654.

[9] 'Basterebbe accennare al fatto che in Isvizzera non esiste il diritto alla parità salariale, la difesa della maternità, non esiste une efficiente rete di asili e di scuole'. Maria Delfina Bonada, Verso una conferenza sull' emigrazione feminile, in *Emigrazione italiana, Organo mensile della Federazione delle Colonie Libere Italiane in Svizzera*, Maggio (1967), 11. See also Maria Delfina Bonada, La donna emigrata, il lavoro, la famiglia, in *Emigrazione italiana, Organo mensile della Federazione delle Colonie Libere Italiane in Svizzera*, Ottobre (1967), 1–2.

[10] Baumann, *...und es kamen auch Frauen. Engagement italienischer Migrantinnen in Politik und Gesellschaft der Nachkriegsschweiz*, Zürich: Seismo 2014, 159.

An Exploratory Interview

I conducted an oral history interview with my mother in 2014 and a follow-up interview in 2018. In the first interview, I requested my mother to describe what she noticed about gender equality when she moved to Switzerland.[11] In the second, I asked her how she felt her experience of migration had shaped her political commitment. The fact that I was interviewing my own mother certainly had a substantial influence on the course of our conversation.[12]

I chose to conduct an exploratory interview, as this makes it possible to combine a biographical interview with a thematic expert interview.[13] In such interviews, the course of the conversation is shaped interactively, so to speak 'step by step'. One of the most important strengths of such an approach is the possibility of switching between the roles of the interested but relatively silent listener, the involved, committed interlocutor and the 'annoying' questioner.

Oral history thus allows us to construct a retrospective interpretation of certain incidents.[14] Interviews of this kind therefore reflect not only how the interviewees experienced historical change, but also how they give their lives meaning in the present, deciding on what to include in and exclude from their account. This, in turn, can differ depending on who is listening.

---

[11] The recordings are in my possession. Both interviews were done in Italian.

[12] Pierre Bourdieu, Die biographische Illusion, *Bios. Zeitschrift für Biograhieforschung und Oral History* 90, 1 (1990), 74–81, 79.

[13] In what follows, see Anne Honer, Das Explorative Interview: zur Rekonstruktion der Relevanzen von Expertinnen und anderen Leuten, *Schweizerische Zeitschrift für Soziologie* 20, 3 (1994), 623-640.

[14] Ulrike Jureit, Authentische und konstruierte Erinnerung - Methodische Überlegungen zu biographischen Sinnkonstruktionen, *WerkstattGeschichte* 18 (1997), 91–101; Robert Perks and Alistair Thomson, *The Oral History Reader*, London: Routledge 1998; Dorothee Wierling, Oral History, in Maurer, *Aufriss der historischen Wissenschaften. Neue Themen und Methoden der Geschichtswissenschaft*, Stuttgart: Reclam 2001, 81–148; Sherna Gluck Berger and Daphne Patai, *Women's Words. The Feminist Practice of Oral History*, New York and London: Routledge 1991.

1 INTRODUCTION   5

'AS IF I HAD MADE A JOURNEY BACK IN TIME'

My mother migrated in 1974, at the age of 25, from a Northern Italian city to a village with a population of 3000 in the Rhine Valley. This area of Switzerland, right at the border with Austria, is known for the prevalence of conservative politics. Here, my father had grown up. Both his father and his mother traced their family genealogy in this village back to at least the seventeenth century. My mother, by contrast, came from the leftist region of Emilia-Romagna. In her city of origin, she participated, as a medical student, in the occupation of a psychiatric clinic. According to her, the student body was very politicised at the time. She also remembered that as a high school student she already experienced situations in which street demonstrations led to confrontations with neo-fascists.

My mother's reason for moving was that she wanted to live with my father, whom she had met in Italy while he was travelling, and not because she was looking for a job abroad. In fact, the medical degree that she was in the process of obtaining ended up not being fully recognised in Switzerland and my mother was not allowed to work in a hospital or to open a practice.

My mother summarised her initial experiences in Switzerland as follows: 'It seemed to me as if I had travelled back in time, I don't know, a hundred or at least fifty years'. According to my mother, the ideas associated with the social movements of 1968 arrived later in Switzerland, and certainly in our village, which had various repercussions. My mother found the Swiss family law of that time absurd—including its consequences for daily life.

For instance, a wife required the signature of her husband when making larger purchases. Once, my mother ordered different skin creams from a local company. The bill was delivered to my father, as the head of the family was generally expected to be the one who pays the bills. My mother had not even given his name; in other words, the employees had gone to the trouble to research it, on the assumption that the male breadwinner would pay.[15] Moreover, in contrast to the situation

---

[15] In this context, I should make a personal remark. As I was writing this section, we received a letter from the tax authorities saying that in order to refund overpaid taxes, the details of our bank account were needed. In addition, the letter stated that that we should indicate either our joint account or my husband's account. A transfer to the wife's account was said to be impossible, even if the refund concerned our joint taxation (I work

in our village, my mother explained that in her home city, a woman with children who went to work was not considered a bad mother, a *Rabenmutter*, as this is called in German. According to her, in the cities of northern Italy, it was more common than in Switzerland for women to do wage-work[16] and, therefore, core time[17] at schools had been implemented already when she was a child. In our village, they still did not exist when I went to school in the 1980s and 1990s, as it was simply taken for granted that mothers would stay at home.

It wasn't just my mother who noticed this. Dinahlee Obey Siering arrived in Switzerland in 1992. She came from Liberia and had lived for two years in Washington, DC, before moving to Switzerland. In an interview, she recounted the following incident: 'Once, when I was with my then sister-in-law, first the eldest child went to school, then the second eldest, and when the youngest left, the eldest was already back. I said: "What the hell is going on here?" and my sister-in-law replied: "Welcome to Switzerland, darling! Here the mother has to stay at home and be available every minute!"'.[18]

A similar statement was also made by Delia Krieg-Trujillo, a lawyer and journalist who immigrated from Bolivia to Switzerland: 'When I came to Switzerland, I was shocked, because there were no core times at school. For me and many other migrant women this was a matter of

full time). When I called the cantonal tax authority in order to complain about this unequal treatment, the administrator confirmed the impossibility of changing this procedure. Later I learned from Franzisca Frania that the equality offices of the city and canton of Berne repeatedly receive complaints about exactly this issue and are trying to find a solution with the tax administration. Statement made by Franzisca Frania in an e-mail, 24 November 2017.

[16] However, Italy as a whole had at the time a high rate of women working as housewives.

[17] In German 'Blockzeiten'.

[18] The paragraph cited ends with the following statement: 'In Africa, too, one is defined as a woman by the children. No matter how many degrees you have, you are simply "the mother of..."' Dinahlee Obey Siering, Ich bin in einem Land aufgewachsen, in welchem die Hautfarbe kein Thema war, in Berlowitz, Joris, and Meierhofer-Mangeli, *Terra incognita? Der Treffpunkt Schwarzer Frauen in Zürich*, Zürich: Limmat Verlag 2013, 132–141, 139.

course back in our country of origin. And still, core times have not been generally introduced. This is structural discrimination!'[19]

My mother also mentioned the case of a Swiss family friend who was a teacher in our village and who lost her job when she got married. Married female teachers were often let go because they were seen as providing unnecessary competition in a tight labour market.

Cooking and Sewing Courses for Girls, Geometry for Boys

Another example that shocked my mother concerned the didactic content of schoolwork itself. When I went to secondary school in the early 1990s, girls were sent to cooking, needlework and sewing courses, whereas the boys were taught geometry and technical drawing. However, pupils wishing to take the entrance examination for high school—i.e. the intermediate level between mandatory schooling and university—needed geometry. Correspondingly, if a girl wanted to take this examination, she had to ask to be admitted to the geometry classes—and this meant that, after the cooking course, she had to rush to the 'boys' lessons.' I hated this domestic education curriculum and above all its claim to being scientific. In fact, it was the only time that a teacher seriously complained about my behaviour in class.

Regarding my background, I was clearly one of the privileged ones—both my parents had a university degree. This was very rare in our village. It comes as no surprise that only a very few girls, at the age of 12, opted for what was, after all, an extra study load. In my class, perhaps three girls attended the geometry lessons. In our cooking lessons, we usually prepared an appetiser, a main course and a dessert, whereas in our family, we only ever ate a little something for lunch. Not being used to such a heavy meal, I almost fell asleep in the geometry lessons that followed.

It is very interesting to analyse the historical contexts that led to the introduction of domestic education in Swiss schools. Many factors that

---

[19] Delia Krieg-Trujillo, Migrant women between concernment, participation and self-determination. Panel-discussion under the guidance of Inés Mateos, FemCities Conference: Migrant Women in European Cities (Basel 2011). Conference documentation, Vienna: 2012, https://www.wien.gv.at/menschen/frauen/pdf/femcities-2011.pdf (1 February 2018).

had a formative influence on the history of Switzerland converged there in an exemplary manner, as we will see.

The discussions on the introduction of female handicrafts and home economics can be followed throughout the nineteenth century.[20] In the so-called poor schools, handicrafts were established as a school subject from the eighteenth century onwards. In turn, cantonal school laws gradually made this subject compulsory in the nineteenth century.[21] On the other hand, a compulsory home economics course was only introduced on a broad scale in the 1940s, but the subject has been taught in various forms since the nineteenth century.[22] Numerous organisations had campaigned for the education of women in domestic work, but the different actors did not always pursue the same goals.

Domestic education was, for instance, part of a comprehensive disciplinary process to instil bourgeois norms in the lower classes. Home economics was supposed to teach order, cleanliness, economy and diligence, and to serve as a means of stabilising a class society.[23] The aim was to keep employees productive and healthy, even at low wages, and to keep the workforce calm. From the example of the hard-working housewife, who is happy to get away with a mere fifteen-hour day, the family will 'get to know work not as a curse but as a blessing'.[24] The family will thus see those who are better off without envy, closing the door to the idea of

[20] Anne-Marie Stalder, Die Erziehung zur Häuslichkeit. Über den Beitrag des hauswirtschaftlichen Unterrichts zur Disziplinierung der Unterschichten im 19. Jahrhundert in der Schweiz, in *Schweizerische Zeitschrift für Geschichte* 34, 3 (1984), 370–384.

[21] Brigit Langenegger, Zur Geschichte des Handarbeitsunterrichts, in Kink and Kuster, *Im Wandel der Zeit: LARWH 1910–1920*, Herisau: LARWH (Lehrerinnen und Lehrer Appenzell Ausserrhoden für Werken und Hauswirtschaft) 2010, 4–15.

[22] Ursi Blosser and Elisabeth Joris, Zwei Fliegen auf einen Streich: Bildung für Haus- und Erwerbsarbeit in den ersten Frauenarbeitschulen der Schweiz, in Barben and Ryter, *Verflixt und zugenäht! Frauenberufsbildung - Frauenerwerbsarbeit 1888–1988*, Zürich: Chronos Verlag 1988, 65–75; Elisabeth Joris, Die Schweizer Hausfrau: Genese eines Mythos, in Brändli, Gugerli, Jaun, and Pfister, *Schweiz im Wandel. Studien zur neueren Gesellschaftsgeschichte. Festschrift für Rudolf Braun zum 60. Geburtstag*, Basel and Frankfurt am Main: Helbing und Lichtenhahn 1990, 99–116.

[23] Beatrix Mesmer, *Ausgeklammert - eingeklammert. Frauen und Frauenorganisationen in der Schweiz des 19. Jahrhunderts*, Basel: Helbing & Lichtenhahn 1988, 182.

[24] Rosina Gschwind, *Koch- und Haushaltungskunde nebst einem Anhang über die Aufgabe der Frau in sozialer, sittlicher und pädagogischer Beziehung*, Bern: K.J. Wyss 1894, 60. My translation.

revolution. An advocate of domestic education wrote in 1893 that more domestic sense would lead the working class to a greater desire to work, greater attachment to employers and more satisfaction with its situation. In his tract on the introduction of compulsory domestic schooling, he argued that the impoverishment of families was not caused by their meagre income, but mainly by the incompetence of housewives: 'The woman does not know how to give the man a pleasant home and drives him to the pub. Badly made coffee, an inadequately cooked or misprepared meal, an unmade bed, a hole in a stocking or gown are factors that can push a country down more than much of what a higher theory believes to be the cause of impoverishment, family breakdown and misery'.[25]

Through domestic education, young women were supposed to learn to keep family maintenance costs as low as possible. At the same time, this was also intended to combat alcoholism and the breakdown of marriage. Order in the house ought lead to order in the state. Bourgeois women, on the other hand, found a publicly recognised field of activity through their commitment to education in home economics. Moreover, they also wanted to rectify the lack of qualified maids, as well as to professionalise and, at the same time, upgrade the status of domestic and thus female work.[26] The working class advocated free home economics lessons as well.[27] The commitment to this kind of education also had to do with the idea that Swiss homes should be prevented from being overrun with 'foreign' maids. Through more efficient household management, the Swiss housewife was supposed to be able to get along without domestic workers.[28] It was sometimes also claimed that Swiss men preferred foreign women as wives because these women were more skilled

---

[25] Otto Wyser, *Die Einführung der obligatorischen Haushaltungsschule*, Olten: Oltener Tagblatt 1893, 6. My translation.

[26] Céline Angehrn and Simona Isler, *Hausarbeit als Beruf – eine Historisierung*, etü – HistorikerInnen-Zeitschrift 2013, 6–9.

[27] Joris, Die Schweizer Hausfrau: Genese eines Mythos, in Brändli, Gugerli, Jaun, and Pfister, *Schweiz im Wandel. Studien zur neueren Gesellschaftsgeschichte. Festschrift für Rudolf Braun zum 60. Geburtstag*, Basel and Frankfurt am Main: Helbing und Lichtenhahn 1990, 99–116, 111.

[28] Rosa Neuenschwander, Die Überfremdung in der Hauswirtschaft, Tagung der Berner Frauen von Stadt und Land, veranstaltet vom Kantonalen Arbeitsamt Bern in Verbindung mit Mitgliedern verschiedener Frauenvereine (Gemeinnütziger Frauenverein, Lehrerinnen-, Hauswirtschaftslehrerinnen- und Arbeitslehrerinnenverein usw.), Bern: Büchler & Co. 1924, 11–18.

in domestic work, which would result in a creeping 'foreignisation' of Switzerland, which had to be prevented.[29]

It was no coincidence that in the political climate before the Second World War, many cantons were prepared to comply with the old demand to make such education compulsory.[30] In the 1930s, the idea was in fact propagated that women and mothers were Switzerland's second army.[31] The able housewife was thus placed at the soldier's side.[32] The preparation of food was thus put at the service of security policy: war-related food shortages were to be avoided, and the percentage of men fit for service was to be increased through a good diet. From this perspective, domestic schooling for girls appears as a counterpart to the military education of boys.

Unequal Opportunities at School

As we have already seen, inequality of educational opportunities was produced by the introduction of these home economics classes, as girls were consequently 'relieved' from other subjects. Only with the equality article of 1995 was such gender-specific discrimination no longer legally permissible.[33]

---

[29] Andrea Althaus, *Vom Glück in der Schweiz? Weibliche Arbeitsmigration aus Deutschland und Österreich (1920–1965)*, Frankfurt am Main: Campus 2017, 79.

[30] Rolf Leemann, *Der Hauswirtschaftsunterricht und seine Integration in die Volksschule unter dem Aspekt seines allgemeinbildenden Wertes*, Fraubrunnen: Selbstverlag 1990, 152.

[31] Eugen Wyler, An unsere Frauen und Mütter! Und ein Wort an die Jugend!, in Schmid-Itten, Meili-Lüthi, and Wyler, *Der Grenzdienst der Schweizerin 1914–1918. Von Frauen erzählt*, Bern: A. Schmid & Cie 1934, 9.

[32] Claudia Crotti, 'Frauen und Mütter sind gleichsam die zweite Armee unseres Landes'. Hauswirtschaft im Dienste der Sicherheitspolitik der Schweiz (1895–1945), in Boser, Bühler, Hofmann, and Müller, *Pulverdampf und Kreidestaub. Beiträge zum Verhältnis zwischen Militär und Schule in der Schweiz im 19. und 20. Jahrhundert*, Bern: Bibliothek am Guisanplatz 2016, 167–189, 167.

[33] Renate Bieg, Zur Geschichte des Hauswirtschaftsunterrichts in Appenzell Ausserrhoden, in Kink and Kuster, *Im Wandel der Zeit: LARWH 1910–1920*, Herisau: LARWH (Lehrerinnen und Lehrer Appenzell Ausserrhoden für Werken und Hauswirtschaft) 2010, 16–29, 27.

1 INTRODUCTION   11

This unequal treatment of girls and boys in Swiss schools has still not undergone comprehensive historical investigation. The reason for this may be that each of Switzerland's today 26 cantons had the authority to create its own curriculum, and each municipality even enjoyed a certain degree of autonomy with regard to school issues. A survey published in 1968 showed that, on average, girls received fewer teaching hours in all subjects relevant for high school entry examinations.[34] For instance, in the canton where I grew up (St. Gallen), boys received 380 more teaching hours in German than girls.[35]

However, it was not only girls who were systematically disadvantaged in their education. For example, when I went to school, all children had to take an examination at the end of grade six, in order to decide who would go to secondary school and who would go to the so-called *Realschule*. Those who entered the *Realschule* had the opportunity to repeat the examination after one year. Most of the children from working-class families were first sent to the *Realschule*. Some passed to secondary school after a year. Only those who attended secondary school could later go on to high school. There were always very few that did so. Children from so-called guest worker families practically didn't attend high school. There was exactly one student with such a background in my high school class. I remember that our secondary school teachers sometimes advised even good students from a so-called migrant background not go to high school. Many people report similar experiences from their childhood.[36] Today, in high schools, the number of female

---

[34] 'L'étude ci-jointe révèle pourtant une situation très claire: la fillette e la jeune fille suisse reçoit, à l'école primaire, une instruction inférieure à celle que reçoit le garçon. La différence entre les programmes est doublement grave dans les années qui précèdent l'entrée au Gymnase ou au Collège puisqu' il y une situation d'infériorité à l'examen d'entrée ou au cours de la première année'. Rolande Gaillard, Enquêtes sur les programmes scolaires, préambule, in Frauenvereine, *Erhebung über die Lehrpläne in den Volksschulen*, 1968, 1–3, 3.

[35] Bund der Schweizerischen Frauenvereine, Erhebung über die Lehrpläne in den Volksschulen, 1968, 132. See also the data for 1977 published in Die Stellung der Frau in der Schweiz. Teil I: Gesellschaft und Wirtschaft. Bericht der Eidgenössischen Kommission für Frauenfragen, Eidgenössische Drucksachen und Materialzentrale 1979, 19.

[36] This semester, my students conducted interviews with politicians with an experience of migration. Discrimination at school was reported several times. Historical research is still lacking in this area.

students has now overtaken the number of male students in all cantons.[37] Nevertheless, only about twenty percent of university professors are women.[38]

Bring to the Fore Not Only Personal, But Also Structural Conditions

Of course, in terms of gender equality, Switzerland was not more backward than other countries in every respect. In this context, the early implementation of a liberal divorce law in Switzerland, for instance, has already been mentioned. In addition, regarding the debate about the use of gender-inclusive language, my mother stated that Switzerland was in fact more progressive than Italy in the 1990s.[39] However, the experiences my mother had when she first moved to Switzerland were an important reason for her engagement in political activities. First, she became part of the local women's group of the Social Democratic Party of Switzerland.[40] For her, this political engagement was a way to get to know people on the same wavelength, since—according to her—there were not many of them where we lived. Later, my mother was elected to the local school board for eight years and to the cantonal parliament for twelve years. She was not aware of any other politicians with dual citizenship in the cantonal parliament at that time. There, she fought for, among other things, a hospital emergency centre for rape victims and for gender-neutral language in laws.

Her experience of migration shaped her political engagement. For example, when it had to be decided how to spread the holidays over the whole year, she knew that long Christmas holidays were important for Italian families, in order to be able to visit their relatives. She was also acquainted with other school models, as both her parents and sisters

---

[37] Janine Hosp and Luca De Carli, Bei der Matur überflügeln die Frauen die Männer, *Der Bund* (24 October 2017), 1.

[38] https://www.sbfi.admin.ch/dam/sbfi/en/dokumente/2017/04/factsheet-hs.pdf.download.pdf/Factsheet_Hochschulen_CH_de.pdf (30 May 2018).

[39] Perhaps these early changes could also be interpreted as a kind of compensation for earlier delays.

[40] My mother made these two statements during the follow-up interview.

worked as teachers in Italy. On her view, longer school days based on the model of a day school were 'not a cruelty to children'. Not everybody appreciated this sort of political engagement. I remember that as a schoolgirl, a friend told me that his parents did not like my mother as a 'foreigner' getting involved with Swiss politics.

It is of course a subjective narrative that my mother presented during the interview. However, similar experiences were also articulated by Irena Brežná, for instance, who moved to Switzerland after the Soviet Union invaded Czechoslovakia.[41] According to the literature, there is in fact a great deal of evidence that in Switzerland, in the boom years after the Second World War, the social and subjective exaltation of the housewife's role was particularly marked.[42] It would be very interesting to carry out a systematic project focusing on different accounts of such experiences. These narratives would of course differ from person to person. For example, moving from a city to a small village or vice versa would, presumably, affect how the specific situation was perceived and, later, described. Such voices, while always individual, allow us to paint a picture of Switzerland's past that until now was seldom part of either Swiss historiography or collective memory. In this way, they bring to the fore not only personal, but also structural conditions. And they would make it possible to capture the political impact of everyday occurrences that are not passed down in other historical sources.[43]

---

[41] 'Das Problem der Schweiz ist ihr Dünkel'. Interview mit Irena Brežná und Blend Hamza http://www.derbund.ch/schweiz/standard/das-problem-der-schweiz-ist-ihr-duenkel/story/12775030 (26 August 2016).

[42] Jakob Tanner and Brigitte Studer, Konsum und Distribution, in Halbeisen, Müller, and Veyrassat, *Wirtschaftsgeschichte der Schweiz im 20. Jahrhundert*, Basel: Schwabe 2012, 639–702, 680; Joris, Die Schweizer Hausfrau: Genese eines Mythos, in Brändli, Gugerli, Jaun, and Pfister, *Schweiz im Wandel. Studien zur neueren Gesellschaftsgeschichte. Festschrift für Rudolf Braun zum 60. Geburtstag*, Basel and Frankfurt am Main: Helbing und Lichtenhahn 1990, 99–116.

[43] Alistair Thomson, Moving Stories: Oral History and Migration Studies, *Oral History* 27, 1 (1999), 24–37.

Open Access This chapter is licensed under the terms of the Creative Commons Attribution-NonCommercial-NoDerivatives 4.0 International License (http://creativecommons.org/licenses/by-nc-nd/4.0/), which permits any noncommercial use, sharing, distribution and reproduction in any medium or format, as long as you give appropriate credit to the original author(s) and the source, provide a link to the Creative Commons license and indicate if you modified the licensed material. You do not have permission under this license to share adapted material derived from this chapter or parts of it.

The images or other third party material in this chapter are included in the chapter's Creative Commons license, unless indicated otherwise in a credit line to the material. If material is not included in the chapter's Creative Commons license and your intended use is not permitted by statutory regulation or exceeds the permitted use, you will need to obtain permission directly from the copyright holder.

CHAPTER 2

Conceptual Clarifications

Abstract This chapter develops the conceptual basis of the book and explains its key terms. History systematically told from a perspective of migration changes national self-perceptions. However, it is not a question of adding a history of migration to so-called general history. Hence, migration should not only be brought to the fore in domains where its influence is obvious. Instead, all fields of society have to be looked at differently: democracy, agriculture, or, as is the case here, gender equality. What we need is a 'migrantisation' of our understanding of the past. Besides introducing key terms and concepts such as 'gender innovation', I explain why this book aims to overcome the often unproductive splitting apart of different forms of mobility that so far have rarely been analysed together.

Keywords Gender innovation · Migrantisation of history · Sedentary bias · Intersectionality · A unified analysis of migration

GENDER INNOVATION

The term 'gender innovation' is sometimes used to describe a gain in scientific knowledge. For instances, in a forthcoming book, entitled *Gender Innovation in Political Science*, the contribution of feminist scholarship to new norms and knowledge in various areas of political science is analysed.[1] My use of the term is different. I understand gender innovation as a subform of sociopolitical innovation in relation to the emergence, implementation or dissemination of new forms of life in different areas of society, but always with reference to a change in gender relations.[2]

I strongly dissociate myself from another use of the concept 'social innovation', namely when it becomes 'a convenient buzzword to forward neoliberal ideology in a time of austerity'.[3] Note that, depending on the perspective of the beholder, innovation doesn't necessarily have a positive connotation—in fact, the term 'social innovation' long had pejorative connotations, describing deviant behaviour and especially socialist doctrines.[4] By choosing this concept, which is today usually positively connoted, I nonetheless intend to reverse the usually negative framing of migration as first and foremost a 'problem'.

The Intersection of Discrimination and Privileges and New Reconfigurations

To understand processes of sociopolitical innovation, the concept of intersectionality is highly important. This term was first coined by Kimberlé Crenshaw in a seminal paper in which she analysed the 'particular manner in which Black women are subordinated'.[5] At the intersection, different kinds of discrimination meet. The resulting oppressive

---

[1] Marian Sawer and Kerryn Baker, *Gender Innovation in Political Science*, Cham: Springer International Publishing (Palgrave Macmillan) 2019. Londa Schiebinger uses the term '*gendered* innovation' in order to describe how a gender analysis can lead to innovation. See for instance http://genderedinnovations.stanford.edu/what-is-gendered-innovations.html (1 February 2018).

[2] Forms of life, in turn, are based on socially shared practices. Rahel Jaeggi, *Kritik von Lebensformen*, Berlin: Suhrkamp 2014, 77.

[3] Francesco Grisoli and Emanuele Ferragina, Social Innovation on the Rise: Yet Another Buzzword in Time of Austerity? *Salute e società* 1 (2015), 169–179, 169.

[4] Benoît Godin, Social Innovation: Utopias of Innovation from c.1830 to the Present (2012), in: http://www.csiic.ca/PDF/SocialInnovation_2012.pdf (12 January 2016).

[5] Kimberlé Crenshaw, Demarginalizing the Intersection of Race and Sex: A Black Feminist Critique of Antidiscrimination Doctrine, Feminist Theory and Antiracist Politics, *The University of Chicago Legal Forum* 140 (1989), 139–167, 140. Even though the term was new, the awareness that categories intersected was not: Marlou Schrover and Deirdre M. Moloney, Introduction. Making a Difference, in: Schrover and Moloney, *Gender, Migration and Categorisation. Making Distinctions Between Migrants in Western Countries, 1945–2010*, Amsterdam: Amsterdam University Press 2013, 7–54, 13. Therefore, one has

effect follows a 'logic' of its own and is not limited to the simple addition of the various forms of discrimination.[6] An intersectional approach thus studies how specific discriminatory effects result from the connection of various kinds of oppression. Crenshaw developed her approach as a critique of how the legal system in the USA reacted to lawsuits where both race and gender discrimination were involved. Accordingly, the focus was on the specific effects of multiple forms of discrimination. Without neglecting the important dimension of discrimination, the concept of intersectionality can also be used in a broader sense,[7] in order to analyse situations where certain privileges intersect with specific ways of discriminating and as a consequence, the potential for new social and political configurations results. It is precisely the coexistence of privileges and discrimination that can generate change, as several examples in this book will show. Intersectionality therefore not only allows the actors of different social movements to realise the 'interconnectedness of the issues that concern them' and in doing so to strengthen their struggle.[8] Even without such an awareness of the actors involved, the intersection of privileges and discrimination can produce a situation that fosters social change, as we will see.

The clash of privileges with specific forms of discrimination has been addressed by different scholars. For instance, Floya Anthias called this 'contradictory locations'.[9] At the end of her article, Anthias also briefly indicates that such situations have a potential for transformation, but she

to be aware that '[c]hoosing this particular point of origin erases the synergy of intersectionality's critical inquiry and critical praxis, and recasts intersectionality as just another academic field'. Patricia Hill Collins and Sirma Bilge, *Intersectionality*, Cambridge: Polity 2016, position 1507–1509 (kindle).

[6] Patricia Purtscher and Katrin Meyer, Die Macht der Kategorien. Kritische Überlegungen zur Intersektionalität, *Feministische Studien. Zeitschrift für interdisziplinäre Frauen- und Geschlechterforschung* 28, 1 (2010), 130–142.

[7] For instance, it has been very convincingly shown that intersectionality does not operate uniquely in the direction of exclusion and that it 'can also be used to understand how women deploy their agency to reverse the disadvantages of socioeconomic position, gender, and ethnicity which initially handicap them'. Yvonne Riaño, Drawing New Boundaries of Participation: Experiences and Strategies of Economic Citizenship Among Skilled Migrant Women in Switzerland, *Environment and Planning* 43, 7 (2011), 1530–1546, 1544.

[8] Collins and Bilge, *Intersectionality*, Cambridge: Polity 2016.

[9] Floya Anthias, Transnational Mobilities, Migration Research and Intersectionality. Towards a Translocational Frame, *Nordic Journal of Migration Research* 2, 2 (2012), 102–110.

does not provide any empirical material to demonstrate this. The concrete examples described in this book shall hopefully take the theory of intersectionality a small step further by analysing such processes very concretely.

A 'Migrantisation' of the Past

History systematically told from a perspective of migration changes national self-perceptions.[10] Such an intention can, however, remain on the level of an empty assertion, if the constitutive dimension of migration is not shown in concrete terms. For it is not a question of adding a history of migration to so-called general history. Migration should therefore not only be brought to the fore where its influence is obvious. Instead, all fields of society have to be looked at differently: democracy, agriculture, or, as is the case here, gender equality. What we need is not primarily a history of migration, which can be found in books that specifically address this topic, but a 'migrantisation' of our understanding of the past. In short, we need a different viewpoint.[11]

Very often, dominant discourses—and not only in Switzerland—suffer from a sedentary bias and thereby produce an unquestioned assumption that migration is per se a problem.[12] If migration is perceived from the point of view of a sedentary bias, then it inevitably becomes something that 'needs to be fixed' by a certain set of policies: 'The repressive variant is tight border control, the more liberal one is addressing the "root causes" of migration—especially poverty and violence in origin

[10] Some of the thoughts I am developing here have already been presented in a very condensed form in the following texts: Francesca Falk, Marignano da, Migration dort, Südafrika nirgends. Über eine gewollte Entkoppelung von Diskursen, *Traverse. Zeitschrift für Geschichte* 3 (2015), 155–165; Francesca Falk, Hat die gegenwärtige Schweiz so wenig mit der vergangenen zu tun? *Wochenzeitung*, 7 January 2016 (2016), 20–21.

[11] In this context, Janine Dahinden makes a plea for 'de-migranticising' migration research while 'migranticising' general social scientific research. Janine Dahinden, A Plea for the 'De-migranticization' of Research on Migration and Integration, *Ethnic and Racial Studies* 39, 13 (2016), 2207–2225.

[12] This was analysed by, among others, Liisa Malkki, The Rooting of Peoples and the Territorialization of National Identity Among Scholars and Refugees, *Cultural Anthropology* 7, 1 (1992), 24–44; Tim Cresswell, *On the Move: Mobility in the Modern Western World*, London and New York: Routledge 2006; Oliver Bakewell, Keeping Them in Their Place. The ambivalent relationship between development and migration in Africa (2007), in: https://www.imi.ox.ac.uk/publications/wp-08-07 (1 November 2016).

countries—so that people do not have to migrate. Either way, migration is seen as harmful and dysfunctional'.[13] The fact that migration often takes place under very problematic conditions should of course not be negated. The 'problem', however, is not migration itself, but rather the enabling conditions of our political and economic system, for instance in regard to the inequality under which most South–North migration takes place.[14]

A sedentary bias can also be found in academic approaches to migration. For instance, in recent essays I have shown how Swiss history has often been written in such a way as to frame migration as, above all, a challenge or problem in need of a solution.[15] As a result, the fundamental way in which migration has shaped contemporary society is overlooked. The relations described in this book between migration and what I call gender innovation thus often go unrecognised. For example, if we look at one of the most recent publications analysing the women's movement in Switzerland, groups formed by 'migrant' women fighting for equal rights are completely ignored. It is as if they were not part of the women's movement.[16] This shows that if we do not start to look at the past from a different perspective, statements, or omissions that are unjustifiable when migration is taken into account, will occur again and again. The Swiss case is not an isolated case. For the USA, the following statement was made in 2001: 'US women's history [...] still has not completely succeeded in conceptualising 'the immigrant woman' into its analysis of the women's movement'.[17]

The *present* struggle for gender equality too has so far mostly been written as one in which migration is seen as a problem. Specifically,

---

[13] Stephen Castles, Understanding Global Migration: A Social Transformation Perspective, *Journal of Ethnic and Migration Studies* 36, 10 (2010), 1565–1586, 1567.

[14] Ibid.

[15] Falk, Marignano da, Migration dort, Südafrika nirgends. Über eine gewollte Entkoppelung von Diskursen, *Traverse. Zeitschrift für Geschichte* 3 (2015), 155–165; Falk, Hat die gegenwärtige Schweiz so wenig mit der vergangenen zu tun? *Wochenzeitung*, 7 January 2016 (2016), 20–21.

[16] This is even more regrettable, as it is otherwise a valuable book: Kristina Schulz, Sarah Kiani, and Leena Schmitter, *Frauenbewegung. Die Schweiz seit 1968. Analysen, Dokumente, Archive*, Baden: Hier und Jetzt 2014.

[17] Christiane Harzig, Women Migrants as Global and Local Agents. New Research Strategies on Gender and Migration, in *Sharpe, Women, Gender, and Labour Migration. Historical and Global Perspectives*, London: Routledge 2001, 15–28, 20.

'migrant' men are seen as causing problems and 'migrant' women as having them—as being a risk and being at risk, as Marlou Schrover aptly puts it.[18] The significance of migration as a possible motor of equal rights is thus erased both from history and the present.

This contribution presents a different picture of the role of migration in Swiss society.[19] Specifically, it analyses distinct but also interrelated fields of research: access to higher education and political rights, the changing gendered division of work and, connected to this, the establishment of a nursery infrastructure. These fields have been selected to show that migration generated gender innovation in various constellations. They allow us to reflect on how, precisely, such processes of migration and emancipatory change occur and how they can be explained. This question will, whenever possible, be addressed by means of an agency-centred approach,[20] while at the same time taking into account those social structures that shape and delimit the possibility of individual and collective action.

THE RELATIONSHIP BETWEEN SPATIAL AND SOCIAL CHANGE

In 1984, a seminal issue on *Women in Migration* was published in the *International Migration Review*. Almost thirty years later, Donna Gabaccia, stated that 'evidence has accumulated that every point in the migration process is gendered'.[21] Despite this important insight,

---

[18] Marlou Schrover, Feminization and Problematization of Migration: Europe in the Nineteenth and Twentieth Centuries, in Hoerder and Kaur, *Proletarian and Gendered Mass Migrations. A Global Perspective on Continuities and Discontinuities from the 19th to the 21st Centuries*, Leiden: Brill 2013, 103–131.

[19] In German, the concept of 'postmigrantism' refers to the idea that today's society is essentially shaped by migration. See for instance Erol Yildiz and Marc Hill, *Nach der Migration. Postmigrantische Perspektiven jenseits der Parallelgesellschaft*, Bielefeld: Transcript 2015. Shermin Langhoff originally coined this term. As artistic director at the Ballhaus-Theater in Berlin (2008–2013), she launched a 'young post-migrant' theatre festival: Kijan Espahangizi, Das #Postmigrantische ist kein Kind der Akademie (2016), in: https://geschichtedergegenwart.ch/das-postmigrantische-kein-kind-der-akademie (2 March 2017).

[20] Damir Skenderovic, Vom Gegenstand zum Akteur: Perspektivenwechsel in der Migrationsgeschichte der Schweiz, *Schweizerische Zeitschrift für Geschichte* 61, 1 (2015), 1–14. Laura Agustin, Forget Victimization: Granting Agency to Migrants, *Development* 46, 3 (2003), 30–36.

[21] Donna R. Gabaccia, Gender and Migration, in Ness, *The Encyclopedia of Global Human Migration*, Malden: Wiley-Blackwell 2013, https://onlinelibrary.wiley.com/doi/book/10.1002/9781444351071 (3 February 2014).

however, many facets of the historical relationship between gender and migration remain unexplored. In showing how migration generates gender innovation in different settings, this study combines a historical perspective with a discussion of timely issues. It brings together a set of case studies, rendering visible their entanglements, and highlighting how the different examples are 'both specific to and representative of a larger phenomenon'.[22] This contribution focuses on the case of Switzerland.[23] Its findings, however, have implications for the understanding of migration and its relation to sociopolitical innovation in more general terms.[24]

Historically, there has been a dichotomy in academic perceptions of migration and social–political change. One school of thought sees 'migrants' as responsible for sustaining the status quo, for example when they are labelled as wage squeezers and strike-breakers,[25] whereas others perceive 'migrants' as natural activists.[26]

Albert O. Hirschman suggested in his famous treatise 'Exit, Voice, and Loyalty' that members of a group can either exit or voice their dissent, i.e. try to change the situation by leaving (exit) or by criticism

---

[22] Michel Wieviorka, Case Studies: History or Sociology? in Ragin and Becker, *What Is a Case? Exploring the Foundations of Social Inquiry*, Cambridge: Cambridge University Press 2000, 159–172, 170.

[23] Recently, numerous new books on the past and present of migration in Switzerland have been published and more will appear in the coming months. Here I will name only a short selection: André Holenstein, Patrick Kury, and Kristina Schulz, *Schweizer Migrationsgeschichte. Von den Anfängen bis zur Gegenwart*, Baden: Hier und Jetzt 2018; Philipp Lutz, *Neuland. Schweizer Migrationspolitik im 21. Jahrhundert*, Zürich: Libro, Neue Zürcher Zeitung 2017; Barbara Lüthi and Damir Skenderovic, *Switzerland and Migration. Historical and Current Perspectives on a Changing Landscape*, Cham: Springer International Publishing (Palgrave Macmillan) 2018.

[24] In this context, see Efremkin. Evgeny, At the Intersection of Modernities: Migrants as Agents of Economic and Cultural Change, *Journal of Contemporary History* 51, 2 (2016), 531–554. The author studies the impact of 'western modernity' represented by immigrants from the USA and Canada on the working and living habits in Finland and Soviet Karelia (the more unexpected influence of returning 'migrants' on North American society is unfortunately not addressed).

[25] See the example given by Stanford Morris Lyman, *Roads to Dystopia. Sociological Essays on the Postmodern Condition*, Fayetteville: University of Arkansas Press 2001, 144.

[26] Gonzague de Reynold, *La démocratie et la Suisse. Essai d'une philosophie de notre histoire nationale*, Bern: Ed. Du Chandelier 1929, 230.

(voice).²⁷ This suggests that, if we transfer this concept to the *sending* country, migration and mobilisation are two mutually exclusive ways of reacting, and that trade-offs exist between exit and voice.²⁸ Interestingly, Hirschman later revised his thesis and acknowledged that the relation between exit and voice does *not* just simply follow a 'hydraulic model', according to which the more pressure escapes through exit, the less is available for voice. Drawing on the historical example of the last phase of the German Democratic Republic Hirschman came to argue that exit can cooperate with voice, voice can emerge from exit and exit can reinforce voice.²⁹ In short, he showed that under certain conditions migration can further rather than obstruct social and political change in the *sending* country.

This strict dichotomy between *either* 'fighting' *or* 'fleeing' has also been criticised by Donna Gabaccia. She points to the fact that 'the word movement has two distinct meanings. On the one hand, movement means mobility or migration [...]. On the other, movement describes the desire for change and the organisations and alliances of people working for change'.³⁰ It is precisely this relationship between spatial and social change that this book analyses. In contrast to Hirschman's work, however, the focus is not exclusively, but predominantly on the *receiving* country.

Migration and Mobility

Not every form of mobility can be called migration. However, the transition between different types of mobility is often fluid. And although the concept of mobility often functions as a generic term and is therefore understood in a broader sense, there is no clear demarcation line

---

²⁷ Albert O. Hirschman, *Exit, Voice, and Loyalty. Responses to Decline in Firms, Organizations, and States*, Cambridge: Harvard University Press 1970.

²⁸ In this context, see also Jeffrey Herbst, Migration, the Politics of Protest, and State Consolidation in Africa, in: 89, 355 (1990), 183–203, 183.

²⁹ Albert O. Hirschman, Exit, Voice, and the Fate of the German Democratic Republic: An Essay in Conceptual History, *World Politics* 45, 2 (1993), 173–202. See also Mark James Miller, *Foreign Workers in Western Europe. An Emerging Political Force*, New York: Praeger 1981.

³⁰ Donna R. Gabaccia, *Militants and Migrants. Rural Sicilians Become American Workers*, New Brunswick: Rutgers University Press 1988, 1.

between migration and mobility in the scientific terminology.³¹ In this book, my aim is not to define terms in a watertight way, but to investigate concretely what political and social effects can be produced by experiences of migration—understood in a broad sense.

In everyday language, migration is often understood as a movement that involves a crossing of national borders. But definitions always act simultaneously as headlights and blinkers. In fact, a now-dominant paradigm frequently leads to a situation where in public debate only cross-border migration and movements of the 'global proletariat' are perceived as migration. Other forms of migration—such as a change of residence for the purpose of tax reduction—are not usually labelled as migration. A bias can therefore also be seen in what is understood by migration in the dominant discourse. Furthermore, migration is nowadays predominantly negatively connoted, often in contrast to mobility.³² This can be seen, for instance, when the movement of expats (usually qualified as white) is called 'mobility', while other kind of movements connected to work are labelled 'migration'—even if the length of stay at the 'new' location is of a similar length.³³ Given the current political situation, I argue that we need to transform the connotations of the term 'migration' rather than replace it.

A UNIFIED ANALYSIS OF MIGRATION

For researchers investigating the effect of migration on the 'established' population, it will at times be necessary in their analysis to separate out 'migrants' from the 'rest of the society', knowing that this is actually an impossible task.³⁴ In this context, the question arises of

---

³¹ Colin G. Pooley, Mobility, in Ness, *The Encyclopedia of Global Human Migration*, Malden: Wiley-Blackwell 2013, http://onlinelibrary.wiley.com/doi/10.1002/9781444351071.wbeghm376/full.

³² Thomas Faist, The Mobility Turn: A New Paradigm for the Social Sciences? *Ethnic and Racial Studies* 36, 11 (2013), 1637–1646, 1640.

³³ Mawuna Remarque Koutonin, Why Are White People Expats When the Rest of Us Are Immigrants? (2015), in: https://www.theguardian.com/global-development-professionals-network/2015/mar/13/white-people-expats-immigrants-migration?CMP=fb_gu (20 October 2015).

³⁴ Mark Terkessidis, *Nach der Flucht: Neue Ideen für die Einwanderungsgesellschaft*, Ditzingen: Reclam 2017.

when and for how long someone may be referred to as a 'migrant'. It can be stigmatising to attach someone to a 'migrant identity' and highly problematic to 'migrantise' people who have long since become part of society.[35] As my approach is not intended to lead to the essentialising of identities, I put the term 'migrant' in single quotation marks. In fact, there is no straightforward distinction between 'locals' and 'non-locals'—nor should such an approach be taken to imply that there was ever something like a pristine, stable world which was then suddenly affected by migration. Since the beginnings of human existence, societies have been shaped by various forms of migration. If many scholars today rightly point out that migration is to be understood as normal in history, we must not, however, lose sight of the consequences of an effective policy of sedentariness. The nineteenth century, for example, is to be seen as a period in which nomadic forms of life came under increasing pressure worldwide due to colonialism. Especially in those moments when the mobility of Europeans increased due to colonial constellations, that of 'travellers' was pathologised, both in the colonial regions and in Europe itself.[36]

The approach envisaged here brings together international as well as internal migration, since it aims to overcome the often unproductive splitting apart of different forms of mobility that so far have rarely been analysed together.[37] It is about thinking processes together that would not otherwise be brought into concert in this way. Precisely this sort of unified analysis is necessary if we want to understand processes of changing gender relations that have been shaped by diverse forms of migration. In this context, Regina Römhild rightly pointed out that only when research focuses on the entire social spectrum of migration can it show that social and political inequality prevails not only between 'migrants' and 'locals', but

---

[35] Regina Römhild, Jenseits ethnischer Grenzen. Für eine postmigrantische Kultur- und Gesellschaftsforschung, in Yildiz and Hill, *Nach der Migration. Postmigrantische Perspektiven jenseits der Parallelgesellschaft*, Bielefeld: Transcript 2015, 37–48, 46.

[36] Jürgen Osterhammel, *Die Verwandlung der Welt*, München: C.H. Beck 2009, 537.

[37] For new mobilities paradigm, see for example Thomas Faist, The Mobility Turn: A New Paradigm for the Social Sciences? *Ethnic and Racial Studies* 36, 11 (2013), 1637–1646; Nina Glick Schiller and Noel B. Salazar, Regimes of Mobility Across the Globe, *Journal of Ethnic and Migration Studies* 39, 2 (2013), 183–200; Mimi Sheller and John Urry, The New Mobilities Paradigm, *Environment and Planning* 38, A (2006), 207–226.

also between different groups of mobile subjects.[38] It is indeed a limited concept of migration that cannot see these major distinctions. Rather, it itself becomes an instrument of the border regime, precisely because it follows the logic of the latter instead of exposing it.

---

[38] Römhild, Jenseits ethnischer Grenzen. Für eine postmigrantische Kultur- und Gesellschaftsforschung, in Yildiz and Hill, *Nach der Migration. Postmigrantische Perspektiven jenseits der Parallelgesellschaft*, Bielefeld: Transcript 2015, 37–48, 42–44.

Open Access This chapter is licensed under the terms of the Creative Commons Attribution-NonCommercial-NoDerivatives 4.0 International License (http://creativecommons.org/licenses/by-nc-nd/4.0/), which permits any noncommercial use, sharing, distribution and reproduction in any medium or format, as long as you give appropriate credit to the original author(s) and the source, provide a link to the Creative Commons license and indicate if you modified the licensed material. You do not have permission under this license to share adapted material derived from this chapter or parts of it.

The images or other third party material in this chapter are included in the chapter's Creative Commons license, unless indicated otherwise in a credit line to the material. If material is not included in the chapter's Creative Commons license and your intended use is not permitted by statutory regulation or exceeds the permitted use, you will need to obtain permission directly from the copyright holder.

CHAPTER 3

Changing Gendered Divisions of Work

Abstract This chapter discusses how migration changed gendered divisions of work. A sedentary bias can also be detected when the gendered effects of emigration from Switzerland are studied. Moreover, when studying emigration, its colonial contexts and, in particular, their relation to gender inequality have to be addressed. In colonial constellations, certain privileges intersected with specific forms of discriminations to produce an ambiguous potential for new social and political reconfigurations. A somewhat similar situation was also created by the migration of nurses from Kerala to Germany, Austria, and Switzerland. Both a sedentary bias and an orientalising way of looking at this kind of migration once again become visible. But such stories could also be told differently, as we will see.

Keywords Changing gendered divisions of work · Sedentary bias · Colonial contexts of emigration · Intersection of privileges and forms of discrimination

Nurses from Kerala

Even though the vast body of secondary literature in migration studies provides a good starting point for reflecting on the reconfiguration of gender relations through migration, this type of scholarship has often focused mainly on the 'migrants' themselves and on the society they *leave*. Those who stay behind, as well as the subjects themselves who move, might perform tasks that do not conform to traditional gender roles (even if this is, of course, not necessarily the case). For example, in a study done on the situation of Italian women in Switzerland, the authors identify important changes in gender relations for Italian couples living in Switzerland: 'In other words, emigration stimulates processes of emancipation. [...] The women reach a certain independence thanks to work and thanks to the confrontation with other models concerning the division of roles'.[1] According to the authors, it was not only 'migrant' women who experienced a process of change. Their male partners now did housework relatively frequently, either because their wives were working or because, having lived on their own in a foreign country, they had learned to get by on their own.[2]

However, the possibility that this kind of migration could also change gender relations in the *receiving* society, i.e., Switzerland at large, is something that has not yet been systematically studied. It is precisely this question that I will look into by analysing the expansion of the nursery infrastructure and its consequences in Chapter 4. For now, let us turn to some interesting special cases concerning the migration of women to Switzerland and its impacts on gender dynamics.

A publication from 1977 on Turkish couples in West Germany suggests that 'in such cases where wives have migrated prior to their husbands, the wife becomes the principal breadwinner and the husband the primary

---

[1] Cristina Allemann-Ghionda, Conclusioni, in *Allemann-Ghionda, Meyer-Sabino, and De Marchi Oechslin, Donne italiane in Svizzera*, Basel: Dadò 1992, 269–288, 269. My translation.

[2] A similar situation was also described with respect to other migration contexts, see, for example, Pierrette Hondagneu-Sotelo, Overcoming Patriarchal Constraints: The Reconstruction of Gender Relations Among Mexican Immigrant Women and Men, *Gender and Society* 6, 3 (1992), 393–415.

However, the care work that is redistributed in sending households in which only women migrate often seems to be performed by female family members, friends or neighbours or outsourced to another 'migrant' woman. Helma Lutz, Gender in the Migratory Process, *Journal of Ethnic and Migration Studies* 36, 10 (2010), 1647–1663, 1654. Sarah Schilliger, Pflegen ohne Grenzen? *Der Privathaushalt als globalisierter Arbeitsplatz*, Bielefeld: Transcript 2019.

child-carer'.[3] However, no empirical data are given to support this claim. Conducting research on 'migrant' couples[4] in which the woman migrated earlier than the man and, as a consequence, had already begun working outside the home before he arrived, therefore seems likely to prove fruitful. In this context, Urmila Goel studied how, in the 1960s and 1970s, Catholic institutions in Germany used their global networks to recruit young Christian nurses from Kerala. Research in Switzerland and the USA[5] has confirmed these findings.[6] After several years of work, most of these women had married highly qualified men from Kerala. However, their husbands could join their wives in West Germany only in the framework of regulations concerning family reunification. Consequently, they were not immediately eligible for work permits and instead stayed home and brought up the children. As a result, the women remained the main breadwinners in these families, while their husbands initially looked after the household and children. Later, these men were often forced to accept occupations below the level of their own qualifications and even those of their wives. The division of work within these families thus differed from the norms in both India and Europe.[7] Here, we see how specific privileges like the right to immigrate intersect with specific forms of discriminations and thereby produce a new configuration.

Urmila Goel showed, moreover, that the existing research on these families focused most often on the resulting problems, for example, cases of alcoholism. It was also assumed that due to India's 'patriarchal

---

[3] Nermin Abadan-Unat, Implications of Migration on Emancipation and Pseudo-Emancipation of Turkish Women, *The International Migration Review* 11, 1 (1977), 31–57, 40.

[4] For same-sex couples, the situation was and still is different, not only in regard to the division of tasks within the family, but also with respect to the right of residence.

[5] Sheba Mariam George, *When Women Come First. Gender and Class in Transnational Migration*, Berkeley: University of California Press 2005.

[6] Many of these nurses apparently travelled from Austria to Switzerland. Simone Gschwend, *Aushandeln transnationaler und lokaler Beziehungen. Eine Fallstudie zu sozialen Netzwerken von Migranten und Migrantinnen aus Kerala, Indien*, Zürich: Ethnologishes Seminar der Universität Zürich 2007.

[7] Urmila Goel, Heteronormativity and Intersectionality as Perspective of Analysis of Gender and Migration: Nurses from India in West Germany, in Poma Poma and Pühl, *Perspectives on Asian Migration: Transformations of Gender and Labour Relations*, Berlin: Rosa-Luxemburg-Stiftung 2014, https://www.rosalux.de/fileadmin/rls_uploads/pdfs/rls_papers/Papers_Asian_Migration.pdf (1 July 2018).

structure', such a role reversal was particularly hard for Indian men to adapt to. However, according to Goel, these stories could also be told in a different way: strong women forged their own path—and their husbands joined in. These Indian nurses could then be regarded as protagonists who were part of the West German emancipation of women.[8] The fact that such a perspective was not, in fact, adopted and that the focus was on the problematic, rather than the productive dimensions of this migration, is the result of both a sedentary bias and an orientalising way of looking at this kind of migration. Here again, conceptualising 'the immigrant woman' into an analysis of the women's movement remains a research desideratum.

Against this background, it would also be of interest to systematically investigate what happened to those couples in which the woman was native to the country and the man came from abroad. For instance, in the family of a friend of mine, the mother was Swiss while the father came from Spain. In this case, the father stayed at home and the mother went to work as long as they lived in Switzerland.[9] In Switzerland in the 1970s and 1980s, such a distribution of roles was still very rare. It would therefore be interesting to study more binational cases in which the father relocated.

A Sedentary Bias in the History of Emigration

At this point, we turn to emigration from Switzerland and its associated gender effects. The region that is now Switzerland experienced intense and sustained emigration for centuries, and it is only since the last decades of the twentieth century that immigration has become more common than emigration. The main focus of this contribution is on migration to Switzerland and its impact on changing gender relations. In future work, it would be worthwhile to address the same question with regard to Swiss emigration.[10] As is the case with most discussions

---

[8] Urmila Goel, Praxis und (Re)Präsentation. (Wieder)Herstellung von Heteronormativität im Migrationskontext (2009), in: http://www.urmila.de/DesisinD/Geschichte/malayali/malluindex.html (1 July 2018).

[9] The family later moved to Spain.

[10] A good starting point is offered by Brigitte Studer, Caroline Arni, Walter Leimgruber, Jon Mathieu, and Laurent Tissot, *Die Schweiz anderswo. AuslandschweizerInnen* -

of immigration, a sedentary bias can, in fact, also be detected when the effects of emigration from Switzerland are studied.

A good example can be found in the interpretation of emigration from what is now called the Canton of Ticino during the early modern period. At that time, the seasonal emigration of men led to local women taking over all the work to be done in their home region. Contemporaries who visited these areas described this in very negative terms and often claimed that, in the absence of men, the whole community developed pathological traits. According to a widespread narrative, a correlation between migration and social stagnation was postulated. In addition, the alleged effects of mothers' working on children's health were described in very drastic terms. According to Paolo Ghiringhelli, for instance, in no other region of Switzerland did one see so many deaf and dumb people as in Ticino.[11] He attributed this to the hard work done by the women, who would often carry the heaviest burdens on their backs uphill and downhill even on the day of their parturition, to the clumsiness of the midwives, and to bad childcare in general. In spring and autumn, the mothers' and the other female members of the family would stay away from the house all day long, leaving the small children to the care of other children who, according to Ghiringhelli, were hardly able to keep themselves upright. Under such circumstances, the children would be in danger of being crushed, burning, falling—or of being eaten in the cradle by pigs, or at least seriously injured by them. In summer, the small children would be taken to the fields. There, they would stay with their heads uncovered, leaving them exposed to the scorching rays of the sun. This would boil their brains and make them into deaf, dumb, and completely stupid people.

As other reports also testify, this kind of migration called into question the traditional division of labour, revealing it to be a social construct rather than a natural phenomenon—which would explain the angry reactions. However, in historical research, the negative opinion expressed in such sources was for a long time simply taken over as is. For instance, Ghiringhelli's statements were not checked, but repeated verbatim, nor

SchweizerInnen im Ausland. La Suisse ailleurs. Les Suisses de l'étranger - les Suisses à l'étranger, Zürich: Chronos 2015.

[11] See, for example, Paolo Ghiringhelli, *Topographisch statistische Darstellung des Cantons Tessin*, Helvetischer Almanach für das Jahr 1812.

was there a discussion of which function such discourses should fulfil.[12] Instead of simply showing how this migration was perceived by contemporaries, historians adopted these opinions as their own and thus, by extension, the view that emigration had reinforced the bad position of women. That a historian who is uncritically attached to his sources, adopts the judgement of contemporary observers and even transfers it to the present day is, under such circumstances, not surprising. For example, the following was written in this context: 'Emigration was not only a mean of stabilising the size of the population, it also stabilised the backwardness from which the Ticino has still not [...] recovered today'.[13]

Only relatively recently have two female historians, Patrizia Audenino and Paola Corti, developed a different view on this process: 'For these reasons, the women of the Alps could have verified precociously how the division of domestic and productive roles was a social construction, rather than a natural phenomenon'.[14] Of course, it is not a question of proclaiming a naive narrative of 'emancipation', since the very difficult living conditions of these women must not be neglected. But only from a perspective like the one adopted by Audenino and Corti can the dimension of migration come into view, which can be an important trigger for socio-political change.

---

[12] A good example is André Schluchter, Die 'Nie Genug zu verwünschende Wuth in Fremde Länder zu gehen.' Notizen zur Emigration der Tessiner in der frühen Neuzeit, in Jaritz and Müller, *Migration in der Feudalgesellschaft*, Frankfurt: Campus Verlag 1988, 239–262; André Schluchter, *Demografia e Emigrazione nel Ticino in Epoca Moderna (secoli XVI–XIX), Col bastone e la bisaccia per le strade d'Europa. Migrazioni stagionali di mestiere dall'arco alpino nei secoli XVI–XVIII*, Bellinzona: Arti grafiche A. Salvioni 1991, 21–48.

For a more detailed discussion on this, see Francesca Falk, Marignano da, Migration dort, Südafrika nirgends. Über eine gewollte Entkoppelung von Diskursen, in *Traverse. Zeitschrift für Geschichte* 3 (2015), 155–165.

[13] Schluchter, Die 'Nie Genug zu verwünschende Wuth in Fremde Länder zu gehen.' Notizen zur Emigration der Tessiner in der frühen Neuzeit, in Jaritz and Müller, *Migration in der Feudalgesellschaft*, Frankfurt: Campus Verlag 1988, 239–262, 258. My translation.

[14] Patrizia Audenino and Paola Corti, Il mondo diviso. Uomini che partono, donne che restano, *L'Alpe* (2001), 12–19, 19. My translation. See also Patrizia Audenino, Introduzione - la dinamica dei ruoli, in Valsangiacomo and Lorenzetti, *Donne e lavoro. Prospettive per una storia delle montagne europee XVIII–XX secc*, Milano: FrancoAngeli 2010, 17–25.

Colonial Constellations

In the colonies, women were also often perceived in ways that diverged from the European image of the 'weaker sex'. The local women appeared to the European colonisers to be workhorses: carrying wood, stomping grain in heavy mortars, carrying heavy loads to the market, and doing 'unwomanly' work in the fields.

It is well known that colonialism legitimised itself as a civilising mission with the aim of improving the position of women in particular. In this context, female missionaries, female professionals, and missionary wives were able to create a field of activity of their own by 'educating' local girls and women and through medical work. Against this background, it appears evident that the colonial contexts of Swiss emigration, and in particular their relation to gender inequality, need to be addressed.[15]

In the case of Bertha Hardegger, for instance, gender discrimination was directly related to her decision to leave Switzerland. Hardegger had studied medicine.[16] When her father died, she took over his practice, but only in order to preserve it for her younger brother, who was just taking his final examinations.[17] In 1936, she left Switzerland for South Africa, and in 1937 she moved to colonial Lesotho, where she became the first female doctor in that region. She was also one of the first female Swiss Catholic missionary doctors. According to Ruramisai Charumbira, 'Hardegger was following the footsteps of many educated European women who found an outlet in the colonies, where they could and did

---

[15] For an analysis of the presence and perseverance of colonial structures and power relations in a country like Switzerland that has not understood itself as an official colonial power, see, for instance, Patricia Purtschert, Francesca Falk, and Barbara Lüthi, Switzerland and 'Colonialism without Colonies.' Reflections on the Status of Colonial Outsiders, *Interventions. International Journal of Postcolonial Studies* 18, 2 (2016), 286–302.

[16] In what follows, see Ruramisai Charumbira, Becoming Imperial. A Swiss Woman's Shifting Identity in British Southern Africa, in Purtschert and Fischer-Tiné, *Colonial Switzerland. Rethinking Colonialism from the Margins*, Basingstoke: Palgrave Macmillan 2015, 157–178.

[17] Bertha Hardegger, Eine junge Frau aus dem Toggenburg wird Missionsärztin: Bertha Hardeggers Lebenslauf, in Specker, *Bertha Hardegger, Mutter der Basuto. Als weisse Ärztin in Schwarzafrika*, Olten: Walter-Verlag AG 1987, 11–16, 12.

become their own mistresses and practiced their professions fully'.[18] Against this backdrop, it comes as no surprise that Hardegger saw the independence of Lesotho in 1966 critically and returned to Switzerland in 1970, where she ran a medical practice in Thalwil.

In colonial constellations, women were considered by the dominant European ideology to be inferior within a race that was considered superior.[19] Therefore, certain privileges intersected with specific forms of discriminations and produced an ambiguous potential for new social and political reconfigurations. Female colonists exercised power over colonised men and were, for instance, able to delegate menial work to them. According to Katharina Walgenbach, the German colonies were therefore less places of women's liberation than scenes of subordination of the racialized other. In her opinion, it can be assumed that racist privilege in the colonies in fact stabilised traditional gender relationships between European men and women, because white women were compensated for their gender discrimination on another level.[20]

A somewhat different picture is drawn in the research on Swiss missions.[21] The relationship between mission and gender innovation is here as well highly ambivalent. Undisputed is that this mission was defined as

---

[18] Charumbira, Becoming Imperial. A Swiss Woman's Shifting Identity in British Southern Africa, in Purtschert and Fischer-Tiné, *Colonial Switzerland. Rethinking Colonialism from the Margins*, Basingstoke: Palgrave Macmillan 2015, 157–178, 157.

[19] Margaret Strobel, Gender and Race in the Nineteenth- and Twentieth-Century British Empire, in Bridenthal, Koonz, and Stuard, *Becoming Visible: Women in European History*, Boston: Houghton Mifflin 1987, 375–396, 375.

[20] Katharina Walgenbach, Emanzipation als koloniale Fiktion: Zur sozialen Position Weisser Frauen in den deutschen Kolonien, in *L'Homme. Europäische Zeitschrift für Feministische Geschichtswissenschaft* 16, 2 (2005), 47–67; Katharina Walgenbach, *'Die weisse Frau als Trägerin deutscher Kultur.' Koloniale Diskurse über Geschlecht, 'Rasse' und Klasse im Kaiserreich*, Frankfurt am Main: Campus 2005.

[21] Compared with the Protestant missions, especially to the Basel Mission, little research has been done on the Catholic mission in Switzerland. Simone Bleuer and Barbara Miller are currently investigating relations, interdependencies and contact zones between Switzerland and colonial Zimbabwe on the basis of the Catholic Swiss Bethlehem Mission Society. With regard to North America, Manuel Menrath showed how Swiss Catholic missionaries moved to the US around the middle of the nineteenth century to proselytise the indigenous peoples living there—above all the Sioux. Manuel Menrath, *Mission Sitting Bull. The Cultural Conquest of the Sioux and Their Varied Response*, Morgantown, PA: Swiss American Historical Society by Masthof Press 2017.

a male enterprise and that the movement behind it embraced conservative views of women's participation in public life.[22] Even when women were designated as missionaries, they were often given subordinate status without the rights held by men.[23] Missions thus often confined women's activities to a limited sphere. On the other hand, in order to create Christian communities, women were indispensable as wives and teachers.[24] Girls were, for instance, taught domestic skills by older women, among other subjects, as they were trained to become Christian wives and mothers.[25] Cleanliness and hygiene campaigns in these years aimed at instructing both Europe's underclass and colonial subjects, while, at the same time, striving to establish bourgeois gender concepts.[26] The aim was to instruct these women so that they would be able to raise their children 'properly'. Colonial policies thus specifically aimed

---

[22] Line Nyhagen Predelli and Jon Miller, Piety and Patriarchy: Contested Gender Regimes in Nineteenth-Century Evangelical Mission, in Huber and Lutkehaus, *Gendered Mission: Women and Men in Missionary Discourse and Practice*, Ann Arbor: The University of Michigan Press 2002, 67–111.

[23] Mary Taylor Huber and Nancy C. Lutkehaus, Introduction: Gendered Missions at Home and Abroad, in Huber and Lutkehaus, *Gendered Mission: Women and Men in Missionary Discourse and Practice*, Ann Arbor: The University of Michigan Press 2002, 1–38, 14.

[24] Nyhagen Predelli and Miller, Piety and Patriarchy: Contested Gender Regimes in Nineteenth-Century Evangelical Mission, in Huber and Lutkehaus, *Gendered Mission. Women and Men in Missionary Discourse and Practice*, Ann Arbor: The University of Michigan Press 2002, 67–111, 77.

[25] Judith Becker, Frauen in der Mission und Mächenschulen, in Christ-von Wedel, *Basler Mission. Menschen, Geschichte, Perspektiven 1815–2015*, 2001, 57–62; Simone Prodolliet, *Wider die Schamlosigkeit und das Elend der heidnischen Weiber. Die Basler Frauenmission und der Export des europäischen Frauenideals in die Kolonien*, Zürich: Limmat Verlag 1987. See also Ulrike Sill, *Encounters in Quest of Christian Womanhood. The Basel Mission in pre- and early colonial Ghana*, Leiden and Boston: Brill 2010; Waltraud Haas, Erlitten und erstritten. Der Befreiungsweg von Frauen in der Basler Mission 1816–1966, Basel: Basilea Verlag 1994; Christine Keim, Frauenmission und Frauenemanzipation. Eine Diskussion in der Basler Mission im Kontext der frühen ökumenischen Bewegung (1901–1928), Münster: Lit Verlag 2004.

[26] Linda Ratschiller is currently working on a PhD project at the University of Fribourg that analyses how the Basel Mission shaped knowledge of hygiene both abroad and at home between 1885 and 1914. See also Linda Ratschiller and Siegfried Weichlein, *Der schwarze Körper als Missionsgebiet. Medizin, Ethnologie und Theologie in Afrika und Europa 1880–1960*, Köln, Weimar, and Wien: Böhlau Verlag 2016.

to change relationships between women, men, and children.[27] In addition, the circumstances created by the colonial constellation often placed pressure on received understandings about differences between men and women and their proper roles among colonised and colonisers alike. The paid employment of women to promote evangelical domestic ideals abroad implicitly violated and thus critiqued those very same ideals. And sending young children home to be reared and educated deprived missionary wives of many of the roles of motherhood. The imperial mission was therefore from its beginning gendered. It left its marks on the division of labour and relations between women and men in the broader societies in which the missions originated, as well as those in which the missions pursued their goal.[28]

---

[27] In what follows, see Huber and Lutkehaus, Introduction: Gendered Missions at Home and Abroad, in Huber and Lutkehaus, *Gendered Mission. Women and Men in Missionary Discourse and Practice*, Ann Arbor: The University of Michigan Press 2002, 1–38.

[28] Nyhagen Predelli and Miller, Piety and Patriarchy: Contested Gender Regimes in Nineteenth-Century Evangelical Mission, in Huber and Lutkehaus, *Gendered Mission. Women and Men in Missionary Discourse and Practice*, Ann Arbor: The University of Michigan Press 2002, 67–111, 70.

Open Access This chapter is licensed under the terms of the Creative Commons Attribution-NonCommercial-NoDerivatives 4.0 International License (http://creativecommons.org/licenses/by-nc-nd/4.0/), which permits any noncommercial use, sharing, distribution and reproduction in any medium or format, as long as you give appropriate credit to the original author(s) and the source, provide a link to the Creative Commons license and indicate if you modified the licensed material. You do not have permission under this license to share adapted material derived from this chapter or parts of it.

The images or other third party material in this chapter are included in the chapter's Creative Commons license, unless indicated otherwise in a credit line to the material. If material is not included in the chapter's Creative Commons license and your intended use is not permitted by statutory regulation or exceeds the permitted use, you will need to obtain permission directly from the copyright holder.

CHAPTER 4

Nurseries

Abstract In the long boom following the Second World War, it was working 'migrant' families and their specific needs that fostered the expansion of a nursery infrastructure. This was not done because mainstream values had changed, but because there was a practical need for such services. Indeed, it can be argued that it was the presence of this infrastructure that, together with other influences, led to a progressive normalisation of nursery childcare in Switzerland. Changing forms of life—whether adopted voluntarily or involuntarily—and the new infrastructure that emerged to cater to these needs assumed a force of their own and, gradually, effected a shift in social attitudes. In order to complete the revised picture of the relation between migration and gender innovation in Switzerland, this chapter ends with an examination of the personnel working in nurseries, this time focusing specifically on male staff members in the present day.

Keywords Nurseries · Infrastructure · Normalising effects · Changing forms of life · Male staff members · The intersection of discrimination and privileges

© The Author(s) 2019
F. Falk, *Gender Innovation and Migration in Switzerland*,
Palgrave Studies in Migration History,
https://doi.org/10.1007/978-3-030-01626-5_4

The First Nurseries

The first institution declared to be a 'nursery' (crèche) was opened in Paris in 1844. In Switzerland, the first city to acquire a nursery was Basel in 1870.[1] Some thirty years later, Bern had six other nurseries and had thus become the leader in the establishment of this kind of infrastructure in Switzerland.[2]

Switzerland was industrialised early on, and its industries relied on female labour. By the middle of the nineteenth century, about half of factory workers were, according to Regina Wecker, women.[3] When the first nurseries were created, medical discourses were extremely influential.[4] It was a declared goal of these institutions to encourage mothers to breastfeed and to teach children and their parents civic hygiene concepts in order to guarantee a healthy and efficient workforce.[5] In this logic, a sterile environment was more important than a stimulating one. In addition, it was considered a central task of these institutions to convey to the working class the bourgeois way of life and due respect for

---

[1] In Switzerland, there are and have been numerous names for the facilities where children from the age of three months are professionally cared for. Not only the terminology but also childcare provision itself varies greatly within Switzerland. It is therefore very difficult to find comparable data and to make corresponding general statements for the whole country. Christine Zollinger and Thomas Widmer, Varieties of Childcare Policies in Swiss Municipalities: Bounded Possibilities for Gender Equality and Social Cohesion, in Liebig, Gottschall, and Sauer, *Gender Equality in Context: Policies and Practices in Switzerland*, Opladen: Barbara Budrich 2016, 111–136.

[2] Katharina Nuspliger-Brand and Alice Marcet, *Der Kindergarten im Kanton Bern. Geschichtliche Darstellung der bernischen Kindergartenbewegung*, Bern: Staatlicher Lehrmittelverlag 1982, 222. Institutions for unattended children from three to six years were established as early as 1828. Anna Bähler and Christian Lüthi, Die vielfältige Bildungslandschaft. Von der Gaumenschule bis zum Kindergarten, in Bähler, Barth, Bühler, Erne, and Lüthi, *Bern - die Geschichte der Stadt im 19. und 20. Jahrhundert. Stadtentwicklung, Gesellschaft, Wirtschaft, Politik, Kultur*, Bern: Stämpfli Verlag AG 2003, 275–276.

[3] Regina Wecker, The Oldest Democracy and Women's Suffrage: The History of a Swiss Paradox, in Charnley, Pender, and Wilkin, *25 Years of Emancipation? Women in Switzerland, 1971–1996*, Bern: Peter Lang 1998, 25–40, 30.

[4] Jean Baptiste Firmin Marbeau, Des crèches, ou, moyen de diminuer la misère en augmentant la population, Paris: 1845.

[5] Ann F. La Berge, Medicalization and Moralization: The Creches of Nineteenth-Century Paris, *Journal of Social History* 25, 1 (1991), 65–87; Catherine Bouve, *L'utopie des crèches françaises au XIXe siècle: un pari sur l'enfant pauvre*, Bern: Peter Lang 2010.

the prevailing conditions in order to prevent political resistance and delinquency.[6] The function of such nurseries was thus also to implant bourgeois values and norms into the working class.[7]

Regarding this first phase, it is still an open question whether the creation of this infrastructure had to do directly with migration. In fact, since it was in Paris that the first public nursery was established in 1844, it cannot be ruled out that people coming to Switzerland from places where nurseries had been created may have acted as brokers in the transnational diffusion of nurseries.[8] In addition, it might have been the case that already at that time 'foreign' children were placed in nurseries more often than their Swiss counterparts. But so far, we do not know for certain.

THE SO-CALLED BOOM YEARS

Be that as it may, the important effect of migration on this process manifests itself at the latest in the so-called boom years. After the end of the Second World War, Switzerland experienced an exceptional economic boom and needed workers from other countries to sustain its high levels of growth.[9] There is an assumption in the literature about this period that post-war migration policies reinforced traditional gender roles. 'Migrants' satisfied the demands of the booming Swiss job market, thus making it possible for the vast majority of Swiss mothers to stay at home

---

[6] Kaspar Burger, A Social History of Ideas Pertaining to Childcare in France and in the United States, *Journal of Social History* 45, 4 (2012), 1005–1025.

[7] Marcello Odermatt, *"Nur unvollkommene Surrogate". Entstehung und Entwicklung und Wandel der Bedeutung und Funktionen von der Kinderkrippe als Fürsorgekonzept. Schweizer Diskurs und Stadtberner Praxis 1870 bis 1950,* Universität Bern: Lizentiatsarbeit Historisches Institut 2005. La Berge, Medicalization and Moralization: The Creches of Nineteenth-Century Paris, *Journal of Social History* 25, 1 (1991), 65–87.

[8] Such a situation can in fact be observed in relation to German refugees in America and England and the establishment of kindergartens: 'In the long run, the suppression of liberalism in the German states after the abortive attempts at revolution in 1848 benefited the kindergarten movement, for it led to a widespread emigration of liberal-minded Germans to America and Western European countries, and in many cases, notably in America and England, the children of these emigrants became the first pupils of kindergartners who were seeking to promote Froebel's ideas beyond the limits of their own country'. Phyllis Woodham-Smith and Evelyn Lawrence, *Froebel and English Education: Perspectives on the Founder of the Kindergarten,* New York: Schocken Books 1969, 24.

[9] A good overview of Switzerland in the twentieth century is given in Jakob Tanner, *Geschichte der Schweiz im 20. Jahrhundert,* München: C. H. Beck 2015.

and take care of their children—or so the argument goes.[10] In this context, we can conceive of the following counterfactual argument: without migration, Swiss women would have been included in the labour market earlier and the use of nurseries would have been adopted more quickly by middle-class Swiss families. However, we cannot know whether this would actually have been the case—or whether there would have been an earlier outsourcing of industrial jobs, for example.

If, on the other hand, we start not from speculation, but from what is given, what do we see when we look with a different perspective at what happened? How can we challenge the assumption that 'emancipation' was prevented in Switzerland because of migration[11]—by highlighting another side of the story? In what follows, I will present some preliminary considerations, which I intend to follow up on in further studies.

THERE IS NEVER A SINGLE STORY[12]

According to a commentary on the 1970 census, three-quarters of the growth in female employment between 1950 and 1960 was due to 'foreigners', and between 1960 and 1970, they were still responsible for

[10] 'Die Einwanderungspolitik der 1950er und 1960er Jahre diente somit gleichzeitig der Durchsetzung des bürgerlichen Familienmodells mit seiner klassischen Rollenverteilung von Alleinernährer und Hausfrau'. Elisa Streuli, Sonja Roest, and Lilo Roost Vischer, Kommen, gehen oder bleiben? Migration in Basel heute, in Ribbert, *In der Fremde. Mobilität und Migration seit der Frühen Neuzeit*, Basel: Historisches Museum 2010, 15–23, 16. 'Die hohe Beschäftigungsquote ausländischer Frauen trug vielmehr dazu bei, die Trennung von Berufs- und Familienarbeit unter den einheimischen Frauen aufrechtzuerhalten'. Sarah Baumann, *...und es kamen auch Frauen. Engagement italienischer Migrantinnen in Politik und Gesellschaft der Nachkriegsschweiz*, Zürich: Seismo 2014, 82. See also Sarah Baumann, Migration, Geschlecht und der Kampf um Rechte. Grenzüberschreitender Aktivismus italienischer Migrantinnen in der Schweiz der 1960er und 1970er Jahre, *Schweizerische Zeitschrift für Geschichte* 65, 1 (2015), 65–82, 74. 'Die Möglichkeit, von einem einzigen Verdienst leben zu können, macht die Erwerbsarbeit der Frauen fakultativ [...]'. Elisabeth Joris and Heidi Witzig, *Frauengeschichte(n). Dokumente aus zwei Jahrhunderten zur Situation der Frauen in der Schweiz*, Zürich: Limmat Verlag 1991 (1986), 78.

[11] 'So zeigt sich, dass die zwei wohl wichtigsten strukturellen Besonderheiten der Schweiz, die Einwanderung von Fremdarbeitern und der Bildungsrückstand, sich beide negativ auf mögliche Emanzipationstendenzen auswirken'. Thomas Held and René Levy, Die Stellung der Frau in Familie und Gesellschaft. Eine soziologische Analyse am Beispiel der Schweiz, 1983 [1974], 38.

[12] On the dangers of single stories, see Chimamanda Ngozi Adichie, The Danger of a Single Story (2009), in: https://www.ted.com/talks/chimamanda_adichie_the_danger_of_a_single_story/transcript?language=en (4 April 2016).

more than half of the increase.[13] Married women were far more likely to work outside the home if they belonged to a 'migrant' family than to a Swiss one.[14] Many migrant women thus had to reconcile the conflicting demands of wage-work and family life well before this question was debated in 'mainstream' Swiss society.[15] At least in the case of Switzerland, therefore, the impact of migration on the development of an infrastructure that made such ways of living possible should not be underestimated.

In post-war Switzerland, there was, in fact, a broad and long-lasting consensus about the temporary character of nurseries. For instance, at its annual meeting in 1964 the president of the *Swiss Nursery Association*[16] stated that nurseries were merely a stopgap for cases in which nursery attendance could not be avoided.[17] And a Swiss encyclopedia published in 1947 confidently stated that nurseries could and should be made largely redundant by higher wages and family allowances.[18] And yet, in

---

[13] Cited from Gaby Sutter, *Berufstätige Mütter. Subtiler Wandel der Geschlechterordnung in der Schweiz (1945–1970)*, Zürich: Chronos 2005, 207.

[14] Werner Haug, *Einwanderung, Frauenarbeit, Mutterschaft. Probleme der schweizerischen Bevölkerungsentwicklung und Bevölkerungspolitik 1945–1976*, Bern: Peter Lang 1978, 63. Katharina Ley, *Frauen in der Emigration. Eine soziologische Untersuchung der Lebens- und Arbeitssituation italienischer Frauen in der Schweiz*, Frauenfeld: Huber 1979. Held and Levy, Die Stellung der Frau in Familie und Gesellschaft. Eine soziologische Analyse am Beispiel der Schweiz, 1983 [1974], 73.

[15] Here, a comparative perspective could be interesting. For instance, it has been showed that in the USA, African-American mothers were more than twice as likely to be employed as white mothers. Elizabeth R. Rose, *A Mother's Job: The History of Day Care, 1890–1960*, New York: Oxford University Press 1999, The same applies to women 'migrants' to the Federal Republic of Germany. Monika Mattes, *"Gastarbeiterinnen" in der Bundesrepublik. Anwerbepolitik, Migration und Geschlecht in den 50er bis 70er Jahren*, Frankfurt am Main: Campus 2005, 82.

[16] In German: *Schweizerischer Krippen-Verband*. Today, this organisation changed its name to *kibesuisse*.

[17] 'Krippen sind und bleiben Notbehelfe', sie sind dann vorgesehen, 'wo der Krippenbesuch nicht abwendbar ist'. Krippenbericht 1964, No. 4, 2–4, 4. Regarding the official gazette of the *Swiss association for nurseries*, see Candid Berz, Der "Krippenbericht". Vereinsorgan des Schweizerischen Krippenvereins (1906–1972). *Beschreibung und Auswertung eines Dokumentes aus einem sozialpädagogischen Tätigkeitsbereich*, Zürich: Lizentiatsarbeit 1974/1975.

[18] Krippen 'sind grundsätzl. ein Notbehelf, der durch höhere Löhne u. Familienzulagen weitgehend überflüssig gemacht werden könnte u. sollte'. *Schweizer Lexikon in 7 Bänden*, Zürich: Encylios-Verlag 1947, 1247.

the post-war period, rising wages and family allowances in Switzerland did not result in a decrease in the number of nurseries—quite to the contrary.

As is the case with any form of historical change, various causes were responsible for turning nursery childcare from an exceptional to a more normal phenomenon in Switzerland. Important factors were, for instance, the so-called new women's movement, which challenged the traditional division of labour, as well as the spread of part-time work as a model for mothers (though not in the same way for fathers).[19] In addition, we should not forget that the golden era of the housewife was in fact a very short one. It was only in the second half of the twentieth century that the ideal of the stay-at-home mother and housewife became a widespread reality in the Swiss working class.[20] In this context, Patricia Purtschert shows brilliantly how the restrictive requirements for women could be enforced by an affective integration of the Swiss housewife into a colonial imaginary. Purtschert outlines how the housewife emerges as the white head of a 'civilised' and consumer-oriented domesticity in constant differentiation from racialised others.[21] Clearly, then, migration is not the only factor that needs to be considered when analysing such complex processes that took place under site-specific

---

[19] Sutter, *Berufstätige Mütter. Subtiler Wandel der Geschlechterordnung in der Schweiz (1945–1970)*, Zürich: Chronos 2005, 257–265. Sarah Schilliger, Umverteilung des 'Krimskrams'. Für eine neue Politisierung feministischer Bedürfnisse (2009), in: http://www.frauenarchivostschweiz.ch/files/olympe/olympe_28.pdf (5 February 2016).
Today, the rate of women who work part-time is higher in Switzerland than in almost any EU country, which is in turn directly linked to a comparatively high level of female employment. However, the high employment rate of women in Switzerland is not comparable with other countries precisely because it does not correspond to a full-time equivalent. According to the 'glass-ceiling index' established by the *Economist* 'aiming to reveal where women have the best chances of equal treatment at work' Switzerland still ranks at the bottom when compared to EU countries. The best—and worst—places to be a working woman (2016), in: http://www.economist.com/blogs/graphicdetail/2016/03/daily-chart-0 (25 July 2016).

[20] Jakob Tanner and Brigitte Studer, Konsum und Distribution, in Halbeisen, Müller, and Veyrassat, *Wirtschaftsgeschichte der Schweiz im 20. Jahrhundert*, Basel: Schwabe 2012, 639–702, 678.

[21] Patricia Purtschert, *Kolonialität und Geschlecht im 20. Jahrhundert. Eine Geschichte der weissen Schweiz*, Bielefeld: Transcript, forthcoming.

conditions.[22] Furthermore, the development of the required nursery infrastructure was not, of course, completed by the end of the economic boom years; rather, this process is still ongoing (witness, e.g., the important decision by the Swiss Parliament, in 2000, to provide start-up funding to new childcare facilities).[23] Even today, there are still long waiting lists in some parts of Switzerland for a place in a nursery and nurseries are often very expensive. Therefore, for some families of the middle class, it is financially attractive to have the mother (who today still often earns less than the father) stay at home. Finally, we should not forget the far-from-easy working conditions in nurseries. This work is nowadays often done by generally very young 'migrant' or second-generation women who have experience of migration in one way or another. For these reasons, it is not a linear success story that I want to tell. There are good reasons not to equate wage labour per se with 'emancipation', especially from a perspective critical of capitalism. Moreover, we have to keep in mind that the working and living conditions of 'migrant' families were not at all easy. These parents often suffered from a particularly heavy workload, because, among other reasons, their own parents lived far away and were thus unable to offer assistance. The women in particular experienced a discrepancy between the role they had internalised and the way they actually lived.[24] Furthermore, female wage labour did not necessarily imply more personal autonomy for women, as female employment does not automatically result in gender equality in the family.[25] It has also been argued that the high regard for wage labour undervalues unpaid care work. As a consequence, some feminists like

---

[22] For instance, it has been argued that in those parts of Switzerland where women worked in the watch-making industry, the benefits of female employment were also emphasised early on by the local elites. Stéphanie Lachat, *Les pionnières du temps. Vie professionnelles et familiales des ouvrières de l'industrie horlogère suisse (1870–1970)*, Neuchâtel: Alphil 2014.

[23] Jacqueline Fehr, Parlamentarische Initiative zur Anstossfinanzierung für familienergänzende Betreuungsplätze (2000), in: https://www.parlament.ch/de/ratsbetrieb/suche-curia-vista/geschaeft?AffairId=20000403 (25 September 2017).

[24] Giovanna Meyer Sabino, Donne in emigrazione, in Halter and Casagrande, *Gli italiani in Svizzera. Un secolo di emigrazione*, Bellinzona: Casagrande 2004, 203–220, 204.

[25] Nelly Valsangiacomo and Luigi Lorenzetti, *Donne e lavoro. Prospettive per una storia delle montagne europee XVIII–XX secc.*, Milano: FrancoAngeli 2010, 11.

Mariarosa Dalla Costa and Silvia Federici called for a different concept of work that could not be reduced to subcontracted work and claimed that housework should pay a wage.[26] Moreover, they criticised the fact that the emancipation of women was often discussed exclusively with regard to female wage-employment and called for an egalitarian division of care work in society. In the Swiss case, it is also important to keep in mind that 'migrant' mothers were often obliged to work, as otherwise their residence permits would expire.[27] Once their situation allowed them to stay at home, this was perceived as a sign of social advancement by some—a phenomenon also observed in the Swiss working class at that time.[28]

Migration and the Development of Nurseries

It is impossible to know how many nurseries were established in these years because they were founded by various entities such as companies, private organisations, and municipalities. However, we can take

---

[26] Silvia Federici, *Wages Against Housework*, Bristol: Power of Women Collective and Falling Wall Press 1975, in: https://caringlabor.wordpress.com/2010/09/15/silvia-federici-wages-against-housework (1 August 2017). See also Nicole Cox and Silvia Federici, *Counter-Planning from the Kitchen. Wages for Housework: A Perspective on Capital and the Left*, Brooklyn, NY: New York Wages for Housework Committee and Falling Wall Press 1975; Silvia Federici, *The Reproduction of Labor Power in the Global Economy and the Unfinished Feminist Revolution, Revolution at Point Zero*, Oakland, CA: PM Press 2012, 91–111; Silvia Federici and Arlen Austin, *The New York Wages for Housework Committee, 1972–1977: History, Theory and Documents*, Brooklyn, NY: Autonomedia 2017. With regard to the Swiss context, see Simona Isler, Lohn für Hausarbeit? Befreiungsperspektiven der Frauenbewegung in den 1970er Jahren, in Bernet and Tanner, *Ausser Betrieb. Metamorphosen der Arbeit in der Schweiz*, Zürich: Limmat Verlag 2015, 216–236.

Mariarosa Dalla Costa had shown already in the 1970s how productive labour is fundamental to the functioning of capitalism. Mariarosa Dalla Costa, *Potere femminile e sovversione sociale con 'Il posto della donna' di Selma James*, Padova: Marsilio 1972.

[27] Saffia Elisa Shaukat, L'approccio di genere alla prova delle migrazioni di stagionali in Svizzera (1949–1973). Questioni di metodo, in Badino and Inaudi, *Migrazioni femminili attraverso le Alpi. Lavoro, famiglia, trasformazioni culturali nel secondo dopoguerra*, Milano: FrancoAngeli 2013, 87–100.

[28] Sutter, *Berufstätige Mütter. Subtiler Wandel der Geschlechterordnung in der Schweiz (1945–1970)*, Zürich: Chronos 2005, 264.

the membership numbers of the *Swiss Nursery Association* (founded in 1907) as a rough indicator for this development.[29] While the association only had 62 members in 1946, by 1961 the number had risen to 90. In 1970, there were already 120 members, and in 1978, membership had grown to 170.[30] In 1970, a book on *The Socio-cultural Problems of the Integration of Italian Workers in Switzerland* was published. According to the author, municipalities were reluctant at that time to tackle the issue of nurseries. As a justification for their attitude, municipal authorities emphasised that this was a task for the employers who had brought in the 'foreigners', that nurseries would encourage mothers to work (which was not perceived as desirable by the municipalities), and that nurseries financed with Swiss tax money would primarily benefit foreign nationals rather than Swiss citizens.[31] And yet, for 'migrant' families, public nurseries were not always the first—or even a realistic—choice. In particular, before 1964, it was often not possible for 'migrants' to obtain a residence permit for their children.[32] If children were allowed to take up residence, they would sometimes live with a Swiss family during the week and stay with their parents only on weekends. One reason for this was that placing one's children with a Swiss family tended to be less expensive than any of the available nurseries. In addition, there were nurseries established by the Italian state and by the *Missione Cattolica*

---

[29] The theoretically conceivable scenario that more nurseries became members—without an increase in the total number of nurseries in the country—seems according to the available data implausible.

[30] Sandra Böhler-Fries, *Zwischen 'Notbehelf' und familienergänzender Institution. Das Deutschweizer Krippenwesen von 1945 bis 1985*, Universität Bern: Lizentiatsarbeit Schweizer Geschichte 2010, 8.

[31] Rudolf Braun, *Sozio-kulturelle Probleme der Eingliederung italienischer Arbeitskräfte in der Schweiz*, Erlenbach: Rentsch 1970, 362.

[32] Martina Marina Frigerio, *Verbotene Kinder. Die Kinder der italienischen Saisonniers erzählen von Trennung und Illegalität*, Zürich: Rotpunktverlag 2014; Martina Marina Frigerio and Simone Burgherr, *Versteckte Kinder. Zwischen Illegalität und Trennung. Saisonnierkinder und ihre Eltern erzählen*, Luzern: Rex 1992. Toni Ricciardi, I figli degli stagionali: bambini clandestini, in Studi Emigrazione and Migration Studies XLVII, 180 (2010), 872–886. See also the ongoing dissertation by Saffia Elisa Shaukat, *Travail temporaire et politiques migratoires en Europe: le cas des 'saisonnier-ère-s' en Suisse (1949–2002)*, University of Lausanne.

specifically for 'migrant' children, in part because some nurseries had to give priority to Swiss families.

At the same time, the actual numbers of 'migrant' children in nurseries show that it was quite common for a high percentage of the nursery clients to be of 'foreign' origin. For instance, when the nursery in Chur was forced to turn down some Italian children in 1964 because of an ordinance by the city, it ended up being undersubscribed, much to the dismay of its staff.[33] Another interesting case is the city of Bern, where, if there was a shortage of places, Swiss children had to be given priority.[34] Nevertheless, the proportion of 'migrant' children in the Swiss capital's nurseries rose to 60–70% by 1965, in part due to the sharp decline in demand for nursery places by Swiss families.[35] In the official gazette of the *Swiss Nursery Association*, various examples of this kind can be found—and this trend is not limited to cities. In more rural Valais, the development of nursery infrastructure is described in 1982 in the following terms: 'At the beginning of the century, the canton was hit by tuberculosis. To help the temporarily orphaned children, the first nurseries were established. Later the problem of single mothers who had to work in order to survive arose. Then the foreign workers arrived. Again new nurseries came into being'.[36] Here too, migration was seen as important for the development of this kind of infrastructure.

This was also the case because, for a very long time, a child was likely to be prevented from attending a nursery if there was insufficient proof that the family depended on the extra income. In the annual report from 1964 of the St. Leonhard nurseries in Basel, for instance, we read: 'In the case of each admission, the material circumstances are […] checked

---

[33] 'Leider hatten wir auch im vergangenen Jahre ein Zurückgehen der Kinderzahlen in Kauf zu nehmen. Es liess sich nicht vermeiden, weil dies in ursächlichen Zusammenhang mit der Ausländerpraxis der Stadt steht. Von einem gewissen Tag auf den anderen durften gewisse Italienerkinder nicht mehr in der Krippe aufgenommen werden'. Krippenbericht 1964 No. 4, 22.

[34] Krippenbericht 1963, No. 4, 12–13.

[35] Krippenbericht 1965, No. 3, 11.

[36] 'Zu Anfang des Jahrhunderts war der Kanton von der Tuberkulose heimgesucht. Um den zeitweise verwaisten Kindern beizustehen, wurden die ersten Krippen gegründet. Später kam das Problem der alleinstehenden Mütter, die, um zu überleben, auswärts arbeiten mussten. Dann kamen die Fremdarbeiter. Wieder entstanden neue Krippen'. Krippenbericht 1982, No. 6, 7.

as accurately as possible, to ensure that really only those mothers will be considered who absolutely need to work'.[37]

The Normalising Effect of an Infrastructure

With the effects of the first and second oil crisis, the situation changed. In the recession years, many 'migrants'—whose residence permits were often dependent on paid employment—had to return to their home countries. Under these circumstances, the established nursery infrastructure became under-used. The editor of the official gazette of the *Swiss Nursery Association*, for example, writes in 1982: 'With the substantial reduction of foreign workers in Switzerland, a further development goes hand in hand: never before in the last, say, 30 years have so many infants coming from middle-class and even well-off circles been found in nurseries as in 1982. This is a reliable sign that children of all social classes meet with universally satisfactory reception in nurseries'.[38] In this statement, the changing social composition of children attending nurseries is both diagnosed and legitimised. Remarkably, the established infrastructure was, in the wake of the oil crisis, opened to a different clientele. The increasing presence of a different clientele went hand in hand with (slowly) changing attitudes towards the nursery 'clients'. Increasingly, in the gazette of the *Swiss Nursery Association* contributions were being published that explicitly refrained from pathologising female work and which tried to take into account that couples had significant leeway in negotiating gender roles.[39] In 1985, for instance, we find an interview with a mother who, like her husband, worked 80%.[40]

---

[37] 'Bei jeder Aufnahme werden [...] die äusseren Umstände möglichst genau geprüft, damit wirklich nur solche Mütter berücksichtigt werden, die unbedingt arbeiten müssen'. Krippenbericht 1964, No. 4, 22.

[38] 'Mit dem substantiellen Abbau der Fremdarbeiter in der Schweiz geht auch eine weitere Entwicklung Hand in Hand: Noch nie waren in den letzten vielleicht 30 Jahren so viele Kleinkinder in Krippen anzutreffen, die aus bürgerlichen und auch gut situierten Kreisen stammen, wie 1982. Das ist ein verlässliches Zeichen dafür, dass Kinder aller Bevölkerungsschichten durchaus in Krippen allseits befriedende (sic) Aufnahme finden'. Krippenbericht 1982, No. 4, 10.

[39] This does not imply that such a change occurred abruptly or without ambiguities. In fact, in the official gazette of the *Swiss Association for Nurseries* such a normalisation is not approved by all from one day to the next.

[40] Krippenbericht 1985, No. 4, 34–36.

In the same year, the example is mentioned of a Finnish mother who was plagued by guilt because she could not find a nursery place for her child.[41] The article describes how she felt her child was being deprived of a valuable experience, and that she feared her offspring would grow up lonely. The readers of the journal of the *Swiss Nursery Association* thus learnt, through the perspective of this Finnish mother, that attending nursery could be assessed in a completely different manner that was common in Switzerland, and that 'because of her socialisation, it was quite simply absolutely normal that children attend a nursery'.[42] In addition, formative experiences of migration can also be found among the staff working for the *Swiss Nursery Association*. For instance, in 1989, the new manager of this association stated that she had lived in Paris und Ghent for several years, and that her experience abroad had taught her 'that day care does not always have to be seen as an "emergency solution" or "substitute", but can be viewed positively in terms of a distinctive educational contribution to the education of young children'.[43] Such a change in mentality was essential for her.

We can thus observe multiple effects of migration on the creation and expansion of childcare infrastructure. In the long boom following the Second World War, it was working 'migrant' families and their specific requirements that fostered the development and expansion of this infrastructure. In the course of these years, nursery infrastructure was not expanded because mainstream values had changed, but because there was a practical need for such services. Indeed, I would argue that it was the presence of this infrastructure that, together with other influences, led to a progressive normalisation of nursery childcare. Hence, it is not only open criticism that served to undermine supposedly incontestable norms and standards. Rather, changing forms of life—whether adopted voluntarily or involuntarily—and the new infrastructure that emerged to cater to these needs assumed a force of their own and, gradually, effected a shift in social attitudes. This is an aspect that has so far been overlooked.

---

[41] Krippenbericht 1985, No. 5, 3–9, here 7.

[42] 'Von ihrer eigenen Sozialisation her ist es eben absolut normal, dass Kinder in die Krippe gehen'. Krippenbericht 1985, No. 5, 3–9.

[43] 'Erfahrungen im Ausland lehrten mich auch, dass eine Krippe nicht immer als 'Notlösung' oder 'Ersatz' betrachtet werden muss, sondern unter dem Aspekt eines eigenständigen, pädagogischen Beitrags zur Erziehung kleiner Kinder positiv gewertet werden darf'. Krippenbericht 1989, No. 4, 9.

The Current Situation

Today, some argue that the outsourcing of care work de facto enables traditional gender roles to be preserved.[44] However, a recent study has shown that, in Switzerland, each newly created afterschool care slot not only motivated mothers to accept a job outside the house, but also encouraged fathers to reduce their paid workload and to assume more childcare duties.[45] Financial support for nurseries in Switzerland—compared to other OECD countries—is still low, and the so-called Male Breadwinner Model is dominant.[46] The employment rate of mothers with children of preschool age has, however, almost tripled since 1980.[47] The proportion of women in wage-work is now high by European standards, as we have seen, but this is mainly because a large number of these women work part-time (and unemployment is generally low in Switzerland).[48] For example, 82.7% of working mothers are not currently in full-time employment. By contrast, fathers are more fully and not less fully employed than their childless peers: almost nine out of ten fathers aged 35–54 are in full-time employment in Switzerland. For men without children of the same age, eight out of ten work full-time.[49] Women who become mothers therefore reduce their paid workload—men who become fathers increase it. This, in turn, has to do with the presence or absence of care structures, as research has shown. According to one

---

[44] See, for example, Mirjana Morokvasic, Gender, Labor, and Migration, in Ness, *The Encyclopedia of Global Human Migration*, Malden: Wiley 2013.

[45] Christina Felfe, Rolf Iten, and Susanne Stern, Child care Services—A Relevant Policy Tool to Enhance Gender Equality? in Liebig, Gottschall, and Sauer, *Gender Equality in Context. Policies and Practices in Switzerland*, Opladen: Barbara Budrich 2016, 199–213.

[46] Rosa von Gleichen and Martin Seeleib-Kaiser, Family Policies and the Weakening of the Male Breadwinner Model (2017), in: https://www.researchgate.net/publication/318745017_Family_Policies_and_the_Weakening_of_the_Male_Breadwinner_Model (6 December 2017).

[47] Francesco Giudici and Reto Schumacher, Erwerbstätigkeit von Müttern in der Schweiz: Entwicklung und individuelle Faktoren (2017), in: http://www.socialchangeswitzerland.ch/?p=1281 (1 November 2017).

[48] Isabelle Stadelmann-Steffen, *Policies, Frauen und der Arbeitsmarkt. Die Frauenerwerbstätigkeit in der Schweiz im internationalen und interkantonalen Vergleich*, Wien: Lit Verlag 2007.

[49] Michael Hermann, Mario Nowak, and Lorenz Bosshardt, Sie wollen beides. Lebensentwürfe zwischen Wunsch und Wirklichkeit (2016), in: https://sotomo.ch/wp/wp-content/uploads/2016/10/Bericht_sotomo_KPT.pdf (18 December 2017).

study, the reduction in the workload of mothers is mainly due to structural factors rather than individual preferences.[50] At the same time, many fathers would like to reduce their paid workload.[51]

In German-speaking Switzerland, the contribution to costs made by parents is generally considerably higher today (2/3 of the full costs) than in French-speaking Switzerland (1/3).[52] In the cantons of Vaud, Fribourg and Neuchâtel, companies are also obliged to co-finance nursery infrastructure via a fund. The question arises as to whether we see here the influence of the respective neighbouring countries on developments in Switzerland, for instance regarding perceptions of motherhood. Especially after 1945, very different political approaches to the expansion of a nursery infrastructure were dominant in the then Federal Republic of Germany and in France. However, there are also major differences within the Swiss language regions. For example, the cantons of Geneva and Vaud have far more nurseries than the other cantons of French-speaking Switzerland. The question therefore arises as to whether such differences map less onto language borders than onto the difference between urban and rural areas.

Male Staff Members with a so-Called Migrant Background

To complete the revised picture of the relation between migration and gender innovation in Switzerland, we will now turn to the personnel working in nurseries, this time focusing specifically on male staff members in the present day.

Today, in various countries, there are attempts to encourage more men to work in nurseries, because as a social institution, it should reflect the diversity of society.[53] In 2015, 2000 people started apprenticeships

---

[50] Ibid.

[51] Inés Mateos, Gleichgestellt? Facts and Figures 2012, in: http://docplayer.org/74131920-Gleichgestellt-facts-figures.html (5 March 2018).

[52] In what follows, see https://www.kibesuisse.ch/fileadmin/Dateiablage/kibesuisse_Publikationen_Deutsch/1505011_Factsheet_Kinderbetreuung_CH.pdf (14 September 2017).

[53] See, for example, The Swiss Project 'More Men in Childcare' http://www.maenner.ch/mehr-maenner-in-die-kinderbetreuung-maki (2 August 2016).

as specialists in nursery childcare in Switzerland, of whom 284 were men.[54] With respect to the background of male apprentices in nurseries, it would be very interesting to obtain accurate statistics, but at least at the moment they are not available.[55] It could be the case that among these male apprentices, the ratio of young men with a so-called migrant background is above average.[56] On the job, these adolescents become important role models and, at the same time, they renegotiate and redefine what masculinity means to them, as they have to find ways to manage 'legitimate subject positions as both childcare workers and as men'.[57] Occupations that are considered as typically female are generally badly paid, and hence, compared to other professions, the remuneration of care work is comparatively low in Switzerland.[58] Young people who are perceived as 'foreigners' (e.g. because they have a name that 'does not sound Swiss') are moreover discriminated against when trying to find an apprenticeship.[59] For example, young people of 'migrant' families of the first generation with comparable formal qualifications to their Swiss

---

[54] http://www.savoirsocial.ch/grundbildung-fachfrau-fachmann-betreuung/zahlen-und-fakten/statistik-fabe-2006-2015.pdf (9 August 2016).

[55] Numbers were requested in vain at the *Federal Statistical Office*, *kibesuisse* and *avenirsocial*.

[56] Interview done with a former manager of a nursery in Basel who was also responsible for coordinating different nurseries, 25 July 2016.

[57] Julia Nentwich, Wiebke Poppen, Stefanie Schälin, and Franziska Vogt, The Same and the Other: Male Childcare Workers Managing Identity Dissonance, *International Review of Sociology* 23, 2 (2013), 326–345, 329. See also Eva Breitenbach, *Männer in Kindertageseinrichtungen. Eine rekonstruktive Studie über Geschlecht und Professionalität*, Opladen: Verlag Barbara Budrich 2015.

[58] Philipp Mühlhauser, *Das Lohnbuch 2016*, Zürich: Orell Füssli Verlag. Franzsika Schutzbach, Who Cares? (2017), in: http://geschichtedergegenwart.ch/who-cares/ (26 June 2017).

[59] Christian Imdorf, Die Diskriminierung 'ausländischer' Jugendlicher bei der Lehrlingsauswahl, in Hormel and Scherr, *Diskriminierung. Grundlagen und Forschungsergebnisse*, Wiesbaden: VS-Verlag für Sozialwissenschaften 2010, 197–219.

According to a new study concerning Switzerland, young men who first express typically male career aspirations and later work in a field that is considered to be typically female seem to dispose of a particularly high level of resources. This is, however, only one subgroup of all those men who work in professions considered as typically female. In

peers have about four times worse chances of finding an apprenticeship.[60] This, in turn, increases the probability that they will finally choose a training position in certain specific professional fields. It is so far an open question whether the tendencies presumed to exist in this study can be proven statistically. In a future project, I would like to investigate this issue. Be that as it may, it seems to be the case that 'gender norms can be shifted and the gendered division of work altered [...] through the combined impact of international migration and of men's employment in feminised paid work'.[61] Here again, certain privileges intersect with specific forms of discriminations and produce once again a quite ambiguous potential for new social and political configurations.

---

addition, the authors point to the small number of these cases in their setting and therefore recommend a cautious interpretation of these figures. Karin Schwiter, Sandra Hupka-Brunner, Nina Wehner, Evéline Huber, Shireen Kanji, Andrea Maihofer, and Manfred Max Bergman, Warum sind Pflegefachmänner und Elektrikerinnen nach wie vor selten? Geschlechtssegregation in Ausbildungs- und Berufsverläufen junger Erwachsener in der Schweiz, *Swiss Journal of Sociology* 40, 3 (2014), 401–428.

[60] Mateos, Gleichgestellt? Facts and Figures 2012, in: http://docplayer.org/74131920-Gleichgestellt-facts-figures.html (5 March 2018).

[61] Ester Gallo and Francesca Scrinzi, Men and Masculinities in the International Division of Reproductive Labour, in *Macmillan, Migration, Masculinities and Reproductive Labour. Men of the Home*, Basingstoke: 2016, 1–36, 30.

Open Access This chapter is licensed under the terms of the Creative Commons Attribution-NonCommercial-NoDerivatives 4.0 International License (http://creativecommons.org/licenses/by-nc-nd/4.0/), which permits any noncommercial use, sharing, distribution and reproduction in any medium or format, as long as you give appropriate credit to the original author(s) and the source, provide a link to the Creative Commons license and indicate if you modified the licensed material. You do not have permission under this license to share adapted material derived from this chapter or parts of it.

The images or other third party material in this chapter are included in the chapter's Creative Commons license, unless indicated otherwise in a credit line to the material. If material is not included in the chapter's Creative Commons license and your intended use is not permitted by statutory regulation or exceeds the permitted use, you will need to obtain permission directly from the copyright holder.

CHAPTER 5

Higher Education

Abstract Switzerland was one of the first countries in the world where women could pursue regular studies at universities open to both sexes. This right to education was not, however, fought for by Swiss women. Moreover, the professors opening the doors for female students were mostly German while the first female professors were of 'foreign provenance'. Once again, the impact of migration on these processes becomes clearly visible. Nevertheless, the impact of these 'foreign' students on Swiss society is often made invisible, as this chapter shows.

Keywords Universities · First female students and professors · Refugees · Invisibilisation · Anti-Semitism · Racism

SWITZERLAND AS A PIONEER—AND WHAT LIES BEHIND IT

Against the backdrop of the aforementioned examples concerning the schooling of girls, it might come as a surprise that Switzerland was one of the first countries in the world where women could pursue regular studies at universities open to both sexes. The possibility of men and women studying together produced important changes in gender relations, an aspect mentioned by the former students Käthe Schirmacher and Svetozar Markovic.[1] This right to education was not, however, fought for by Swiss women. It is a well-known fact that women from the Tsarist Empire (of different nationalities, among them many of Jewish origin) were the pioneers in this struggle.

In the years 1867–1914, between 5000 and 6000 women from the Tsarist Empire studied in Switzerland.[2] At the University of Zurich, the first Swiss university to allow women to attend, the professors opening the doors for female students were, moreover, mostly German.[3] In fact, with regard to the early introduction of co-education in Swiss universities, we have to consider that 'the role of Switzerland as a country which granted political asylum influenced the political climate in favour of women's emancipation'.[4] Once more, it becomes evident that it is not enough to exclusively focus on women—and, for instance, forget the male professors involved—when studying processes of changing gender relations.

The first woman to obtain a doctoral degree was Nadeschda Suslowa in 1867. It is important to realise that, initially, only very few Swiss women made use of their right to study at a university. After the departure of the female students from the Tsarist Empire (numbers peaked

---

[1] Käthe Schirmacher, *Zürcher Studentinnen*, Leipzig and Zürich: Th. Schröter 1896. Peter Brang, Zuflucht der Musen. Slavische Kunst und Kultur im Schweizer Exil, in Bankowski, Brang, Goehrke, and Zimmermann, *Asyl und Aufenthalt. Die Schweiz als Zuflucht und Wirkungsstätte von Slaven im 19. und 20.* Jahrhundert, Basel, Frankurt am Main: Helbling & Lichtenhand 1994, 275–315, 286.

[2] Daniela Neumann, *Studentinnen aus dem Russischen Reich in der Schweiz (1867–1914)*, Zürich: Hans Rohr 1987, 14. Franziska Rogger and Monika Bankowski-Züllig, *Ganz Europa blickt auf uns! Das schweizerische Frauenstudium und seine russischen Pionierinnen*, Baden: Hier und Jetzt 2010, 27. Natalia Tikhonov, *La quête du savoir. Etudiantes de l'Empire russe dans les universités suisses (1864–1920)*, Genève: Université de Genève 2004.

[3] Thomas Ernst Wanger, Vom Frauenstudium zum Frauenwahlrecht in der Schweiz und in Liechtenstein, *Schriften des Vereins für Geschichte des Bodensees und seiner Umgebung* 122 (2004), 117–157.

[4] Regina Wecker, The Oldest Democracy and Women's Suffrage: The History of a Swiss Paradox, in Charnley, Pender, and Wilkin, *25 Years of Emancipation? Women in Switzerland, 1971–1996*, Bern: Peter Lang 1998, 25–40, 30.

around 1910), it took several decades before a comparable level of female enrolment was reached.⁵ Nevertheless, the impact of these 'foreign' students on Swiss society is often made invisible, as the following examples will show.

THE OFT-OMITTED IMPACT OF THESE 'FOREIGN' STUDENTS

Marie Heim-Vögtlin became the first female physician born in Switzerland. Today, she is seen as an icon of women's emancipation, as she managed to reconcile work and family, stood up for female suffrage and co-founded the country's first gynaecological hospital. The *Swiss National Science Foundation* named a scholarship after her, and for the hundredth anniversary of her death in 2016, a Swiss postage stamp was dedicated to her. However, the particular circumstances of her career choice are often omitted, as is the case, for instance, in the *Historical Dictionary of Switzerland*.⁶ It was, in fact, when her fiancé broke off their engagement in 1867 and, soon after, married the aforementioned Nadeschda Suslowa that Marie Vögtlin decided that she too wanted to become a physician.⁷ In the *Historical Dictionary of Switzerland*, however, Marie Heim-Vögtlin's entry lacks any reference to Suslowa. In addition, in the entry on Nadeschda Suslowa it is stated that, as a pioneer, she was a role model for many Russian women who studied in Switzerland in the period leading up to the First the First World War. Her influence on Marie Heim-Vögtlin, the first female Swiss physician, is once again omitted.⁸ The importance of migration as a motor of equal rights is thus erased from history. This is not an

---

⁵Without female students from the Tsarist Empire, equality at the universities progressed much more slowly.

⁶Regula Ludi, Heim [-Vögtlin], Marie http://www.hls-dhs-dss.ch/textes/d/D9330.php (4 July 2016).

⁷Verena E. Müller, *Marie Heim-Vögtlin - die erste Schweizer Ärztin (1845–1916). Ein Leben zwischen Tradition und Aufbruch*, Baden: Hier und Jetzt 2007, 41.

⁸Heinrich Riggenbach, Suslowa, Nadeschda http://www.hls-dhs-dss.ch/textes/d/D31805.php (1 Febraury 2017).

isolated case; other similar examples concerning these two women could be mentioned.[9]

Despite the importance for Heim-Vögtlin of her Russian role model, in 1870, together with five other female students, she urged the rectorate to restrict the conditions for the admission of women, fearing an influx of politicised Russians who, in her eyes, would damage the image of all female students.[10] The request was not successful, but, shortly thereafter, a new university regulation required a Baccalaureate certificate from everyone enrolling at the University of Zurich.[11] Due to the lack of corresponding schools for women at the time, this made access to the university more difficult for them.

Feminist Forerunners Are not Unequivocal Heroines of History

Of course, not only left-wing revolutionaries like Rosa Luxemburg and Alexandra Kollontai studied in Switzerland.[12] M. Carey Thomas, for instance, gained her doctorate at the Philosophical Faculty of the University of Zurich in 1882, the first woman to do so in the Humanities at that university. Incidentally, when, as a student, she fell ill

---

[9] Claudia Wirz, Marie Heim-Vögtlin (1945–1916), in Parzer Epp and Wirz, *Wegbereiterinnen der modernen Schweiz. Frauen, die die Freiheit lebten*, Zürich: Neue Zürcher Zeitung 2014, 71–74.

[10] Schweizerischer Verband der Akademikerinnen, *Das Frauenstudium an den Schweizer Hochschulen. Les études des femmes dans les universités suisses*, Zürich: Rascher 1928, 289.

[11] See for example Müller, *Marie Heim-Vögtlin - die erste Schweizer Ärztin (1845–1916). Ein Leben zwischen Tradition und Aufbruch*, Baden: Hier und Jetzt 2007, 84.

[12] According to Alexandra Kollontai, her consciousness of the revolutionary aims of the working movement emerged in Switzerland. It was while she was studying economics at the University of Zurich that she became familiar with the history of the labour movement. Later, in the Soviet Union, she drafted important pieces of legislation concerning maternity insurance. As Soviet Ambassador to Norway, she was, moreover, one of the first women to be in such a position. Sending her abroad as a diplomat was, however, also a possible way of politically sidelining an influential woman who had become an internal critic of the Party and whose claims in favour of women's right of sexual choice were viewed with great suspicion. Alexandra Kollontai, Alexandra Kollontay. Ziel und Wert meines Lebens, in Kern, *Führende Frauen Europas. In sechzehn Selbstschilderungen*, München: Reinhardt 1929, 258–286.

shortly before her Ph.D. defence, she was successfully treated by Marie Heim-Vögtlin, who was, according to Thomas, 'the most prominent woman doctor here'.[13] Thomas became a pioneer in women's education, the first female college faculty member in America to hold the title of dean, the second president of the Bryn Mawr College and a leading member of the *National American Woman Suffrage Association*.[14] She pursued relationships with other women and never married. When, in 1922, the *New York Times* asked many experts to name the twelve greatest American women, almost all chose to include her on their list.[15]

Before coming to Zurich, Thomas had been refused a Ph.D. at the University of Leipzig and Göttingen because she was a woman. However, the experience of being a victim of prejudice did not alter her own racist worldview. For instance, in letters she wrote from her travels, she denigrated the Japanese as 'radically unintelligent' and Egyptians as 'untrustworthy, untruthful mongrel races, totally ignorant, superstitious and without any intellectual curiosity'.[16] This example demonstrates very clearly that these feminist forerunners are not always unequivocal heroines of history, but sometimes deeply ambivalent figures. Moreover, the case of Thomas also contradicts the naïve claim that geographical mobility necessarily broadens one's mind.

The First Female Full Professor in Switzerland—Born in the Russian Empire

The first female professor in Europe was Sofja Kowalewskaja who became—under special conditions—an extraordinaria in Sweden in 1884 and a full professor in 1889. Her pioneering role as a female mathematician made her the subject of several books.[17] By contrast, little work has

---

[13] Cited from Müller, *Marie Heim-Vögtlin - die erste Schweizer Ärztin (1845–1916). Ein Leben zwischen Tradition und Aufbruch*, Baden: Hier und Jetzt 2007, 192.
[14] Helen Lefkowitz Horowitz, *The Power and Passion of M. Carey Thomas*, New York: Alfred A. Knopf 1994.
[15] Ibid.
[16] Ibid.
[17] See for instance Ann Hibner Koblitz, *A Convergence of Lives. Sofia Kovalevskaia: Scientist, Writer, Revolutionary*, New Brunswick: Rutgers University Press 1993.

been done so far on the first female university professors in Switzerland, except for the interesting research carried out by Natalia Tikhonov Sigrist and Franziska Rogger.

From the moment when Swiss universities opened their doors to women until the beginning of the Second World War, 72% of the 43 female teachers (among them very few professors) were of 'foreign provenance', and half of them had been born in the Tsarist Empire.[18] In this context, it has to be remembered that in Switzerland, it was (and still is) very common for male professors to be of 'foreign' provenance, although the percentage is likely to have been lower than in the case of female professors.

In Switzerland, the first full female professor was Sophie Piccard who became an ordinaria in 1943/44 at the University of Neuchâtel.[19] She had been born in Saint Petersburg. Her mother came from a French Huguenot family (her mother also had a Danish father) and her father from a Swiss family living in Russia. The family was hit hard by the political unrest following the Bolshevik Revolution and the war. A sister died due to the consequences of malnutrition, a brother disappeared. In 1925, the family fled to Switzerland.

In Switzerland, Sophie Piccard's degree was worthless and she had to earn another one from the University of Lausanne. After her Ph.D., she was unable to find a teaching position. Wishing to devote herself to teaching, she undertook pedagogical training, but, in contrast to the Soviet Union, Neuchâtel at that time did not allow women to teach mathematics at the secondary level. Therefore, she worked for an

---

[18] Natalia Tikhonov, Das weibliche Gesicht einer 'wissenschaftlichen und friedlichen Invasion.' Die ausländischen Professorinnen an den Schweizer Universitäten vom Ende des 19. Jahrhunderts bis 1939, in Duchhardt, *Jahrbuch für Europäische Geschichte*, München: Oldenburg 2005, 99–117. Natalia Tikhonov, Zwischen Öffnung und Rückzug. Die Universitäten der Schweiz und Deutschland angesichts des Studentinnenstroms aus dem Russischen Reich, in Peter and Tikhonov, *Universitäten als Brücken in Europa. Studien zur Geschichte der studentischen Migration*, Frankfurt am Main: Peter Lang 2003, 157–174.

[19] In what follows, see Simon Moreillon, Sophie Piccard (1904–1990), in Adler, Parzer Epp, and Wirz, *Pionnières de la Suisse moderne. Des femmes qui ont vécu la liberté*, Genève: Slatkine 2014, 159–163; Natalia Tikhonov Sigrist, Deux Suissesses de l'étranger, pionnières de la féminisation du corps professoral universitaire: Elsa Mahler et Sophie Piccard (2008), http://www.penthes.ch/wp-content/uploads/lettres/ldp011.pdf (24 May 2018).

insurance company and later for a newspaper. In 1936, she was called upon to replace, as a lecturer, a sick professor from the Department of Geometry at the University of Neuchâtel. Her teaching qualities having been recognised, she became an extraordinary professor of higher geometry in 1938. Her career culminated with an appointment, in 1944, to the chair of ordinary professor of higher geometry, probability calculus, and actuarial sciences, which she held for nearly thirty years. In parallel to this engagement, she founded and directed the 'Centre for Pure Mathematics' in Neuchâtel starting from 1940. Her research was carried out at an impressive pace, and she quickly became an authority in her field.

After her mother's death in 1957, she devoted much time and many resources to the publication of her mother's literary and historical writing. Eulalie Piccard's work touched above all on Russian literature, history, and the transformation of Russia into the Soviet Union. Thanks to Sophie Piccard's tenacity, her mother's personal papers, correspondence, works, literary papers, iconographic documents, and press clippings are preserved in the Swiss National Library. These, along with Sophie Piccard's own written legacy, are still waiting for a thorough historical reappraisal.[20]

The scientific, political, social, and cultural potential for innovation of the research done by these early female academics has barely been explored.[21] Moreover, tracing the biographies and legacies of the first female professors would likely be highly rewarding. Studying these cases in-depth would mean analysing their career paths, migration trajectories, and the networks that led these women to work at Swiss universities as well as their impact within their fields and beyond. As this research has not yet been carried out, I will limit myself to describing two other prominent cases, the trajectories of the first female professors in German- and French-speaking Switzerland, respectively.

---

[20] https://www.helveticarchives.ch/detail.aspx?ID=937977 (24 May 2018). Sophie Piccard's own written legacy is located at the City Library in La Chaux-de-Fonds: http://biblio.chaux-de-fonds.ch/bvcf/patrimoine/archives-fonds-speciaux/archives-personnelles/Pages/sophie-piccard.aspx (24 May 2018).

[21] Bettina Vincenz, *Biederfrauen oder Vorkämpferinnen? Der Schweizerische Verband der Akademikerinnen (SVA) in der Zwischenkriegszeit*, Baden: Hier und Jetzt 2011, 172.

The First Extraordinara in Romandie—Born in the Russian Empire

Lina Stern, who was born in present-day Latvia into a German-speaking Jewish family, was named extraordinara in Biochemistry at the University of Geneva in 1918.[22] After Stern's unsuccessful attempt to acquire a full professorship in Geneva, she left for the Soviet Union in 1925 and became a professor in Moscow. In 1932, she was nominated to the famous German *Academy Leopoldina* and, in the same year, received significant research funds from the *Rockefeller Foundation*. Stern was also the first female member of the *Russian Academy of Sciences*.[23] She became famous, among other things, for her ground-breaking work on the blood–brain barrier. In 1943, she won the Stalin Prize. In the same year, she was asked to dismiss two co-editors of a scientific journal, as it had been decided to greatly reduce the number of Jewish physicians in leading positions. Outraged, Stern sent a letter to Stalin and succeeded in preventing a change in the composition of the editorial staff. Her career ended abruptly, however, during the Stalinist purges. It is now known that she was co-accused in the secret military trial of fourteen leading members of the former 'Jewish Anti-Fascist Committee'. She was charged with being a rootless cosmopolitan and sentenced to death. Probably because of her prominent reputation, her punishment was commuted to a prison term. In 1949, she was incarcerated and spent 44 months in prison, followed by a period in exile that was intended to last five years. In 1953, shortly after the death of Stalin, she was released. Before and after this dramatic experience, she maintained an extensive correspondence with her former colleagues from Geneva—a correspondence that still awaits a more thorough study.[24]

---

[22] In what follows, see Jean-Jacques Dreifuss and Natalia Tikhonov, Lina Stern (1878–1968): Physiologin und Biochemikerin, erste Professorin an der Universität Genf und Opfer stalinistischer Prozesse, *Schweizerische Ärztezeitung/Bulletin des médecins suisses/Bollettino dei medici svizzeri* 86, 26 (2005), 1594–1597.

[23] Lina S. Stern, in Kern, *Führende Frauen Europas. Neue Folge in fünfundzwanzig Selbstschilderungen*, München: Reinhardt 1930, 137–140.

[24] Some of these letters are stored at the *Archive of the Russian Academy of Sciences* (holding 1565).

The First Extraordinara in German-Speaking Switzerland—Again Born in...

In 1909, nine years before Lina Stern, the philosopher Anna Esther Pavlovna Tumarkin, of Jewish origin and born in 1875 in what is now Belarus, had become an extraordinara at the University of Bern. Paid only as a lecturer, Tumarkin was the first woman in Europe to have the right to supervise Ph.D.s and review habilitations. However, she was denied appointment to a full professorship, on the grounds of her gender, among other things.[25]

Anna Tumarkin explained philosophy in its historical contexts and analysed life from philosophical, theological, anthropological, and psychological perspectives.[26] In 1937, Tumarkin was awarded the *Theodor Kocher Price* for her philosophical work and in 1999/2000, a path was named after Tumarkin in Bern. It is located to the north of the main university building and is only 90 metres long. So much for the space of recognition that is granted to important women in the Swiss capital. The tribute to the first female professor in Switzerland is almost an insult.

Tumarkin had studied in Bern from 1892 to 1895. After her Ph.D., she went to Berlin for a three-year research stay with Wilhelm Dilthey and other professors. Afterwards, she stayed in the Canton of Bern until her death in 1951. During and after the Second World War, Tumarkin witnessed many of her family members being deported and killed.[27] In

---

[25] Franziska Rogger, *Der Doktorhut im Besenschrank. Das abenteuerliche Leben der ersten Studentinnen - am Beispiel der Universität Bern*, Bern: eFeF-Verlag 1999; Franziska Rogger, *Anna Tumarkin*, Bern: Universitätsarchiv Bern 2000; Franziska Rogger, Anna Tumarkin (1875–1951) - erste Professorin Europas, in Martig, *Berns moderne Zeit. Das 19. und 20. Jahrhundert neu entdeckt*, Bern: Stämpfli Verlag 2011, 448–449; Rogger and Bankowski-Züllig, *Ganz Europa blickt auf uns! Das schweizerische Frauenstudium und seine russischen Pionierinnen*, Baden: Hier und Jetzt 2010.

[26] Monika Kneubühler, Anna Esther Tumarkin. Die Philosophin als jüdische Denkerin, *Judaica. Beiträge zum Verstehen des Judentums* 73, 2/3 (2017), 221–233, 228; Judith Jánoska, Die Methode der Anna Tumarkin, Professorin der Philosophie in Bern, in Arni, Glauser, Müller and Rychner, *Der Eigensinn des Material: Erkundungen sozialer Wirklichkeit. Festschrift für Claudia Honegger zum 60. Geburtstag*, Frankfurt am Main: Stroemfeld 2007, 151–168; and Heinrich Barth, *Zur Erinnerung an Anna Tumarkin und ihr philosophisches Lebenswerk*, Basel: Sonderdruck 1951.

[27] *State Archive of the Canton Bern*, N Tumarkin 1/2, letter of her nephew Moura Konstantinowky alias Georges Constantin, 22 October 1945.

1918, when Kishinev passed to Romania, Tumarkin became stateless. This prompted her to apply for naturalisation. In 1921, she became a Swiss citizen. Her application for naturalisation shows the precarious financial conditions under which these first female professors usually worked. When asked whether she had any savings, Anna Tumarkin wrote in August 1921: 'I have no savings, since I have only recently received a salary from which I can finance my living expenses'.[28] The documents also show that in 1921, she earned 450 francs per year and that she had to pay 300 francs for her new citizenship.

As a student, Tumarkin had reflected upon her not always easy experiences as a 'foreigner' in Switzerland in the draft of a letter to her professor: 'Then I went abroad and here I got to know real loneliness, I often missed sympathy and that's why I understood how to appreciate it'.[29] Interestingly, Tumarkin's most important academic mentor and promotor—and probably also the person to whom this letter is addressed—was professor Ludwig Stein.

Stein was also a 'migrant'. He had been born in what is now Hungary. He studied in Germany and became a professor in Bern. In 1909/1910, he had to resign from his chair because of an anti-Semitic campaign. The reason for the defamatory attack was Stein's harsh criticism of race theories. His opponents represented a racist, anti-Semitic, and misogynist attitude. For example, one opponent found it unbelievable that Stein had the conviction that whoever migrated to America from the Russian Empire at the age of ten to twenty would become an unmistakable Yankee after a few years.[30] When Ludwig Stein died in 1930, Tumarkin wrote an obituary in the newspaper *Der Bund*. She paid tribute to his 'so successful academic work' in Bern—and did not mention his dismissal.[31]

From 1921, Anna Tumarkin lived communally with Ida Hoff. In their wills, the two friends had nominated each other as heiresses, and both

---

[28] *State Archive of Canton Bern*, Dossier 3756/21, Polizeidirektion des Kantons Bern an den Regierungsrat des Kantons Bern zuhanden des Grossen Rates, BB 4.1.1199. My translation.

[29] This document is available at the *State Archive of the Canton Bern*, N Tumarkin 1/2. My translation.

[30] Markus Zürcher, *Unterbrochene Tradition. Die Anfänge der Soziologie in der Schweiz*, Zürich: Chronos 1995, 142.

[31] Anna Tumarkin, Ludwig Stein, in *Der Bund. Organ der freisinnig-demokratischen Politik. Eidgenössisches Zentralblatt und Berner Zeitung* (Universitätsbibliothek Bern, MUE Singer XII Sbd 4: 15), 16 June 1930, (1930), 1.

were buried in the same grave after their death. Such communities were not uncommon among working female academics.[32]

Hoff, too, had experienced migration. She was born in Moscow and came to Switzerland with her mother in 1886.[33] Remarkably, it was once again Ludwig Stein who helped Hoff and her mother to become Swiss citizens. Ida Hoff was one of the first women to be allowed to drive a car in Bern and also the first female school doctor there. In addition, she had been engaged in the women's student association and, for many years after, sat on the board of the *Women's Suffrage Association* of Bern. Anna Tumarkin also advocated the right to vote for women and in 1928, she participated in the *First Swiss Exhibition for Women's Work* (SAFFA). In this context, she co-authored a list of publications by Swiss women, also including some women of 'foreign' origin living in Switzerland.[34] In addition, she wrote several newspaper articles in favour of women's suffrage.[35]

As was the case elsewhere, several of the first female students and professors in Switzerland later became key figures in the struggle for political participation, gender justice, and women's rights—and many of them had experienced some form of migration. Early female academics were, in fact, regularly at the forefront of feminist thought, and it was often the case that the women's student association was a veritable training ground for the female suffrage movement.[36] This brings us to our last topic, the long struggle for female suffrage in Switzerland and its interrelation and interdependency with migration.

---

[32] Vincenz, *Biederfrauen oder Vorkämpferinnen? Der Schweizerische Verband der Akademikerinnen (SVA) in der Zwischenkriegszeit*, Baden: Hier und Jetzt 2011, 51.

[33] In what follows, see Franziska Rogger, Kropfkampagne, Malzbonbons und Frauenrechte. Zum 50. Todestag der ersten Berner Schulärztin Dr. med. Ida Hoff, 1880–19521, *Berner Zeitschrift für Geschichte und Heimatkunde* 64, 3, (2002), 101–119.

[34] Anna Tumarkin and Julia Wernly, *Verzeichnis der Publikationen von Schweizerfrauen*, Bern: Benteli 1928.

[35] Anna Tumarkin, Das Stimmrecht der Frauen, in Der Bund. *Organ der freisinnig-demokratischen Politik. Eidgenössisches Zentralblatt und Berner Zeitung* (Universitätsbibliothek Bern BeM ZB Log X 411: 24), 13 November 1928 (1928); Anna Tumarkin, Wie sind Sie Stimmrechtlerin geworden?, in Berna (Universitätsbibliothek Bern BeM ZB Log X 411: 26), 23 Febraury 1929 (1929).

[36] Wecker, The Oldest Democracy and Women's Suffrage: The History of a Swiss Paradox, in Charnley, Pender, and Wilkin, *25 Years of Emancipation? Women in Switzerland, 1971–1996*, Bern: Peter Lang 1998, 25–40, 31.

Open Access This chapter is licensed under the terms of the Creative Commons Attribution-NonCommercial-NoDerivatives 4.0 International License (http://creativecommons.org/licenses/by-nc-nd/4.0/), which permits any noncommercial use, sharing, distribution and reproduction in any medium or format, as long as you give appropriate credit to the original author(s) and the source, provide a link to the Creative Commons license and indicate if you modified the licensed material. You do not have permission under this license to share adapted material derived from this chapter or parts of it.

The images or other third party material in this chapter are included in the chapter's Creative Commons license, unless indicated otherwise in a credit line to the material. If material is not included in the chapter's Creative Commons license and your intended use is not permitted by statutory regulation or exceeds the permitted use, you will need to obtain permission directly from the copyright holder.

CHAPTER 6

Female Suffrage

Abstract Even if the history of female suffrage in Switzerland is well documented in many respects, its relation to migration has never been systematically analysed. This chapter shows how some of the most prominent figures in the struggle for female suffrage were connected to experiences of migration. It also discusses the example of a woman who lost her citizenship because she married a 'foreigner' and shows why it is heuristically productive, when studying migration, to take such experiences into account. In addition, the connections between women's right to vote in cultural memory and its interrelation to migration are brought to the fore. In this context, the chapter points out that it could be a productive undertaking to systematically investigate how, in Switzerland, women with an experience of migration played a formative role in the establishment of women's and gender history. Moreover, I discuss what the invitation of twelve Nigerian students in 1958 had to do with the invisibilisation of democratic deficits in Switzerland and how this can be historically connected to fighting women in Nigeria and Switzerland.

Keywords Female suffrage · The intersection of discrimination and privileges · Indirect experience of migration · Cultural memory · The establishment of women's and gender history · Unseen democratic deficits

© The Author(s) 2019
F. Falk, *Gender Innovation and Migration in Switzerland*,
Palgrave Studies in Migration History,
https://doi.org/10.1007/978-3-030-01626-5_6

Female Suffrage in Switzerland and Its Relation to Migration

Whereas Switzerland was, as we have seen, a pioneer in making higher education accessible to women, we will now examine Switzerland as an extreme latecomer in another domain. Even if the history of female suffrage in Switzerland is well documented in many respects, its relation to migration has never been systematically analysed. The present chapter will show how some of the most prominent figures in the struggle for female suffrage were related to experiences of migration (and more cases await further analysis).[1]

Historians have long noted the seeming paradox that Switzerland introduced universal male suffrage very early, but female suffrage very late.[2] Switzerland has a system of semi-direct democracy, a factor that has (often without further reflection) been held responsible for this exceptionally late adoption of female suffrage. It was—so the argument goes—because the majority of men had to vote on female suffrage that it proved so difficult to pass. Even if in those days some groups of men were still excluded from political participation (e.g. Jews and those dependent on financial assistance), it has to be acknowledged that in Switzerland the right to political participation—or not—followed gender lines comparatively early on.[3] Later, this was also an important

---

[1] See, for instance, the biographies of Maria Eugster-Breitenmoser, Lotti Ruckstuhl, Annie Reineck, Pauline Chapponnière-Chaix, Auguste de Morsier, Georgine Emma Gerhard, or Dora Schmidt. See SVF, *Der Kampf um gleiche Rechte*, Basel: Schwabe 2009.

[2] Sibylle Hardmeier, *Frühe Frauenstimmrechtsbewegung in der Schweiz (1890–1930). Argumente, Strategien, Netzwerk und Gegenbewegung*, Zürich: Chronos Verlag 1997; Sibylle Hardmeier, Die Vereine in der Deutschschweiz und die Gründung des schweizerischen Verbandes, in SVF, *Der Kampf um gleiche Rechte*, Basel: Schwabe 2009, 67–78; Brigitte Studer, Das Frauenstimm- und -wahlrecht in der Schweiz 1848–1971. Ein 'Fall' für die Geschlechtergeschichte, in Braunschweig, *'Als habe es die Frauen nicht gegeben'. Beiträge zur Frauen- und Geschlechtergeschichte*, Zürich: Chronos 2014, 179–196; Yvonne Voegeli, *Zwischen Hausrat und Rathaus. Auseinandersetzungen um die politische Gleichberechtigung der Frauen in der Schweiz 1945–1971*, Zürich: Chronos Verlag 1997; Franziska Rogger, *'Gebt den Schweizerinnen ihre Geschichte!' Marthe Gosteli, ihr Archiv und der übersehene Kampf ums Frauenstimmrecht*, Zürich: NZZ Libro 2015. See also Beatrix Mesmer, *Ausgeklammert - eingeklammert. Frauen und Frauenorganisationen in der Schweiz des 19. Jahrhunderts*, Basel: Helbing & Lichtenhahn 1988.

[3] Caroline Arni, Republikanismus und Männlichkeit in der Schweiz, in SVF, *Der Kampf um gleiche Rechte*, Basel: Schwabe 2009, 20–31.

handicap to the introduction of female suffrage, as the reform of the political system became a women-only affair.[4] At the national level, women gained the right to vote in 1971, while in some cantons female voting rights were withheld even longer, the last canton being Appenzell Innerrhoden, which finally was forced to introduce female suffrage in 1990 by the Swiss Federal Court.

THE FIRST FORMAL ASSOCIATION PROMOTING POLITICAL AND LEGAL EQUALITY FOR WOMEN

The first formal association promoting political and legal equality for women was established in Geneva in 1868 by Marie Goegg-Pouchoulin as part of an international movement for peace. She was also the initiator of the petition that successfully opened the doors for women at the University of Geneva in 1872.[5] Her ancestors were French Huguenots who had fled to Switzerland after the revocation of the Edict of Nantes. Both her grandfather and her father were watchmakers, an occupation known for its association with socialist and anarchist ideas. When she was already married and the mother of a little boy, she met some refugees of the 1848 Revolution, who had rented rooms in her parents' house. She fell in love with Amand Goegg, one of the leaders of the uprising in Baden (Germany), and demanded a divorce from her husband. As he did not consent, legally they were merely separated. In 1851, Amand Goegg was expelled from Switzerland and went to Paris and later to London. Afterwards, he lived again in Geneva, probably illegally. In 1853, Marie Pouchoulin realised that she was pregnant. Under adventurous circumstances, both travelled to London, taking Marie's now seven-year-old son with them. We do not know how she experienced this stay in London. But it seems very probable that it was there that her interest in

---

[4] Regina Wecker, Staatsbürgerrechte, Mutterschaft und Grundrechte, *Schweizerische Zeitschrift für Geschichte* 46, 3 (1996), 383–410.

[5] In what follows see Susanna Woodtli, *Gleichberechtigung. Der Kampf um die politischen Rechte der Frau in der Schweiz*, Frauenfeld: Huber 1983, 24–49. Mesmer, *Ausgeklammert - eingeklammert. Frauen und Frauenorganisationen in der Schweiz des 19. Jahrhunderts*, Basel: Helbing & Lichtenhahn 1988, 88–93, 102–110. Ruth Nattermann, Frauen in der europäischen Friedensbewegung. Die Association Internationale des Femmes (1868–1914) (2015), in: http://www.europa.clio-online.de/site/lang__de/ItemID__744/mid__11428/40208214/default.aspx (12 January 2016).

feminism grew. In her novel *Deux poids et deux mesures*, she developed her first emancipatory ideas—tellingly through a female character who is English. Moreover, the name she chose for the organisation she founded in order to fight for equal rights, the *Association Internationale des Femmes*, testifies to the extent to which had been inspired by the *International Workingmen's Association* founded 1864 in London. Her idea of establishing clubs providing specialised reading also derived from there.

Migrating Political Strategies

Marie Goegg-Pouchoulin's diverse experience of migration was far from a unique case. Iris von Roten (1917–1990) became an icon of Swiss feminism by publishing a provocative book at the time of the first national plebiscite on female suffrage in Switzerland in 1959. Two experiences of migration were crucial for her.[6] First, there was a case of internal migration—and such internal migration is often neglected in historical research—from one of the biggest cities in Switzerland to a rural area, which led to an intensive experience of discrimination. Iris von Roten was the first female lawyer in the canton of Valais, and clients did not want to be represented by a woman. In addition, von Roten lived in the USA for a year, where she conceived and drafted her soon-to-become notorious book *Frauen im Laufgitter*.[7]

Not only her writing benefited from her experience abroad, but also the political strategies that she and her husband employed in campaigning for female suffrage.[8] In 1957, the women of Unterbäch, a small mountain village in the Swiss canton of Valais, were allowed to participate in a national referendum on the question of whether civil defence service should become mandatory for Swiss women. The chairman of the municipality and the *Nationalrat* (i.e. federal representative) for the Canton of Valais, Peter von Roten—the husband of Iris von Roten[9]—were the initiators of what, at the time, was perceived as a scandal.

---

[6] In addition, a very important research stay in Oxford ought to be mentioned.

[7] Iris Roten, *Frauen im Laufgitter. Offene Worte zur Stellung der Frau*, Bern: Hallwag 1958.

[8] Regina Wecker, Travelling Strategies, Travelling Women: Iris von Roten's Swiss Book, in Pender and Burns, *Crossing Frontiers: Cultural Exchange and Conflict. Papers in Honour of Malcolm Pender*, Amsterdam: Editions Rodopi 2010, 163–184.

[9] Wilfried Meichtry, *Verliebte Feinde. Iris und Peter von Roten*, Zürich: Ammann 2007.

They argued that the village community was legally authorised to set up its voting register. The women's votes were, however, collected in a separate ballot box and never formally counted. Nevertheless, this procedure generated considerable attention, and even the *New York Times* sent correspondents to report from this village of 400 inhabitants.

Interestingly, the Unterbäch strategy looked a lot like the approach American women had pursued in their campaign to gain the vote. According to Regina Wecker, Iris von Roten had studied the American women's struggle 'and may have come across that strategy which seemed so exotic in a small place in the Swiss mountains'.[10]

THE LAST STRAGGLERS

Small spaces are also characteristic for our last examples, in which we analyse the special situation in the two cantons of Appenzell Innerrhoden and Appenzell Ausserrhoden. The predominately Catholic Appenzell Innerrhoden, with approximately 16,000 inhabitants today, and the largely Protestant Ausserrhoden, with currently about 54,000 inhabitants, were the last two Swiss cantons to introduce female suffrage. It was only in 1989 that the male citizens of Appenzell Ausserrhoden narrowly voted for women's suffrage in the traditional *Landsgemeinde*, an annual open-air assembly of all (until 1990 only male) citizens, where public voting on cantonal matters was—and still is in Appenzell Innerrhoden—conducted by a show of hands.

For this canton, the most iconic figure of women's suffrage movement is considered to be Elisabeth Pletscher (1908–2003).[11] She had been raised in Appenzell Ausserrhoden and was the great-great-granddaughter of the *Landammann* (Chairman of the Canton) Jacob Zellweger-Zuberbühler (who had even been invited to Napoleon's coronation).[12] This family was involved in textile and colonial trade activities throughout

---

[10] Wecker, Travelling Strategies, Travelling Women: Iris von Roten's Swiss Book, in Pender and Burns, *Crossing Frontiers: Cultural Exchange and Conflict. Papers in Honour of Malcolm Pender*, Amsterdam: Editions Rodopi 2010, 163–184, 178.

[11] Elisabeth Pletscher received an honorary doctorate degree from the University of St. Gallen in 1998. Renate Bräuniger, Elisabeth Pletscher (*1908) - kein Mangel an öffentlicher Resonanz, in Bräuniger, *FrauenLeben Appenzell. Beiträge zur Geschichte der Frauen im Appenzellerland*, Herisau: Appenzeller Verlag 1999, 424–441, 431.

[12] Hans Fässler, *Reise in Schwarz-Weiss. Schweizer Ortstermine in Sachen Sklaverei*, Zürich: Rotpunktverlag 2005, 46.

the world. Pletscher herself grew up in modest circumstances, as her father died when she was five. She was one of the first girls in the local high school and would have liked to study medicine, but for financial reasons this was not possible.

According to her, she questioned the exclusion of women from the *Landsgemeinde* for the first time as an 18 years old.[13] At that time, a Polish woman, who was married to one of her cousins, opened her eyes. This woman had come to Switzerland during the First World War, had studied there, and was now following her husband to the USA. At the farewell in the village square in Trogen, she explained to Elisabeth Pletscher that she was happy to be able to leave Switzerland, because it was a provincial backwater. She told Pletscher that in Poland, women had already had the vote for a long time. Pletscher responded placatingly that women's suffrage would eventually be introduced in Switzerland, and that only here it might not be possible because of the cantonal assembly. 'That conversation has stayed with me, I remember where we stood. She answered: "But why not?!" "Because it's only for men", was my argument. "And why not for you?" She continued, "you also go to a school with lots of boys and why should you not participate like this later in polls and elections?" It suddenly dawned on me. I thought she was right'.

In addition to this encounter, Pletscher's own migration experience was decisive for her political engagement. She had in fact spent her whole professional life as a chief laboratory technician at the Women's Hospital Zurich. After her retirement, she returned to her birthplace in 1973, and consequently lost the right to vote at the cantonal level, which she had had in Zurich. This experience had a lasting effect on her political engagement. Elisabeth wrote in 1973: 'Personally, I have recently been demoted from a full-citizen in the Canton of Zurich to a 2/3 citizen in the Canton of Appenzell'.[14]

---

[13] In what follows, see Hanspeter Strebel and Kathrin Barbara Zatti, *'Es gibt Dinge, die brauchen Zeit'. Elisabeth Pletscher, Zeitzeugin des 20. Jahrhunderts*, Herisau: Appenzeller Verlag 2005, 91.

[14] 'Persönlich bin ich von einer Voll-Bürgerin im Kanton Zürich seit kurzem zurückversetzt worden in eine 2/3-Bürgerin im Kanton Appenzell'. Elisabeth Pletscher, *Rückblick auf selbsterlebte 'Emanzipation der Frau'*, *Mitteilungen des Kantonsschulverein Trogen*, Trogen: Eigenverlag 1973, 42–45, 44.

In 2004, Julia Nentwich conducted a series of in-depth interviews with individuals who had acted as agents of change in both cantons. A male activist for female suffrage explained to Nentwich that, before going to the *Landsgemeinde*, Pletscher always very consciously wore a traditional costume, and that she then used to speak in her most pronounced local dialect (whereas on other occasions, her dialect was less marked).[15] What we see here is a prototypical situation in which the necessary impulses for change came from the outside. At the same time, they needed to be perceived as coming from the inside in order to be seen as legitimate.[16]

We can find a similar situation in the even more conservative Appenzell Innerrhoden. As late as 1990, the (Swiss) men residing in the canton rejected female suffrage at the cantonal—as opposed to the federal—level at the *Landsgemeinde*. By consequence, a constitutional complaint was brought before the Swiss Federal Court, which eventually declared this treatment of women to be unconstitutional, thus overruling the men's decision. In her interview with Nentwich, a woman active in the *Action Committee for Women's Suffrage* in Appenzell Innerrhoden stated that the initiator of the first legal action,[17] Theresa Rohner, had moved from Appenzell Ausserrhoden to Innerrhoden. As a result of her political involvement, Theresa Rohner also received death threats. According to the interviewee, it was possible only for an 'outsider' to get involved in something like this: '[S]he was capable of doing it, that's my personal theory, because she was not from Innerrhoden [...]'.[18] Here, we see that great importance can be attributed to an experience of migration that took place on a very small scale.

---

[15] "Bewusst hat sie an der Landsgemeinde die Tracht angezogen, obwohl sie jetzt keine Bauersfrau ist, aber sie hat dann die Tracht angehabt und hat dann ihren Appenzeller Dialekt (gesprochen). Sie ist sehr sprachbegabt, sie konnte auch umstellen, sie konnte mehr oder weniger 'appenzellern'" Julia C. Nentwich, Zwischen Provokation und Anpassung: Handlungsmächtigkeit als diskursive Positionierung (2009), in: http://www.qualitative-research.net/index.php/fqs/article/view/1197 (1 July 2016).

[16] Ibid.

[17] Later, there were other legal actions.

[18] Julia C. Nentwich, Mustafa F. Ozbilgin, and Ahu Tatli, Change Agency as Performance and Embeddedness: Exploring the Possibilities and Limits of Butler and Bourdieu, *Culture and Organization* 21, 3 (2015), 235–250, 245.

An Indirect Experience of Migration

A good ten years earlier, in 1978, the pioneering attempt to establish a political women's group campaigning for political rights in Appenzell Innerrhoden had been initiated by Ottilia Paky-Sutter.[19] Some seventy women met at the founding event for a female suffrage association. But Paky's goal to have native women, preferably with a rural background, appear in newspaper advertisements asking for female suffrage, in order to refute the assertion that only newcomers wished political rights, was not achieved.

Ottilia Sutter belonged to one of the most well-known local families. They owned an inn where the 'intelligentsia' of Appenzell met. During the Second World War, she and her sister performed at the national exhibition *Landesausstellung* aimed at strengthening Swiss national identity. From then on, the two singing sisters were seen as paragons of local traditions, and therefore, it comes as no surprise that, in 1945, when General Guisan[20] visited Appenzell, they were chosen to pose for a photograph with him. Just a few years later, the situation changed completely. In 1947, Ottilia Paky-Sutter lost her Swiss citizenship because she married an Austrian. By contrast, if a Swiss man married a 'foreigner', the wife would at that time automatically become a Swiss citizen. Brigitte Studer has brilliantly explained these procedures in her essay on practices and controversies surrounding the special legal treatment of women according to their marital status. In contrast to male citizens, the civic membership of Swiss women was in fact a contingent one.[21]

In 2014, I interviewed the daughter of Ottilia Paky-Sutter. According to her, the decisive factor for her mother's engagement on behalf of female suffrage was the very fact that she had lost her Appenzell, as well as her Swiss, citizenship due to her marriage.[22] Paky regarded this

---

[19] In what follows, see the highly interesting article by Vreni Mock, Ottilia Paky-Sutter (*1918) - eine Österreicherin fordert das Stimmrecht, in Bräuniger, *FrauenLeben Appenzell. Beiträge zur Geschichte der Frauen im Appenzellerland*, Herisau: Appenzeller Verlag 1999, 408–415.

[20] During the Second World War, Henri Guisan held the office of the General of the Swiss Armed Forces.

[21] Brigitte Studer, Citizenship as Contingent National Belonging: Married Women and Foreigners in Twentieth-Century Switzerland, *Gender & History* 13, 3 (2001), 622–654.

[22] Statement made by her daughter in a personal conversation, 23 December 2014: "Was eigentlich den Ausschlag gab, dass sie für das Frauenstimmrecht kämpfte, war, dass sie das Appenzeller und Schweizer Bürgerrecht verloren hatte mit ihrer Hochzeit".

change as a social demotion. The whole family had to become naturalised again, a humiliating and costly procedure for them. It was this kind of indirect migration experience that provoked her political engagement for women's political rights. Again, certain privileges intersected here with specific forms of discriminations and produced a situation where new political reconfigurations became possible—in this case, the political engagement for female suffrage.

This last example of a woman who lost her citizenship because she married a 'non-national' shows that it can be heuristically productive, when studying migration, to include those experiences that do not involve any actual physical movement. I am convinced that such an approach can be highly rewarding, as such processes are most often neglected. By redressing this bias, we are able to rethink the implications of migration more broadly. For instance, in Switzerland today, fewer than 50% of marriages are concluded between Swiss citizens,[23] and this has a decisive impact on society as a whole. Paying particular attention to such indirect migration experiences thus allows us to see how migration policies affect far more people than those who are usually considered as 'migrants'. In this context, however, it is important to stress that this does not mean losing sight of specific privileges or forms of discrimination, quite the opposite.

NOT DOWNPLAYING THE EFFECTS OF RACISM

On my understanding, using a broad concept of migration in fact means the opposite of being blind to differences. We should not downplay the effects of racism or of different legal situations. Therefore, it is always necessary to acknowledge distinctions between various kinds of relocations—for example, with regard to the legal status or racialising categories.

Tilo Frey, for instance, was one of ten women elected as a Swiss National Councillor in the first national election after the introduction of female suffrage in 1971.[24] She had been born in Maroua as the daughter

---

[23] http://www.bfs.admin.ch/bfs/portal/de/index/themen/01/06/blank/key/05/01.html (15 August 2016).

[24] On the involvement of women in political parties after 1971, see Fabienne Amlinger, *Im Vorzimmer zur Macht? Die Frauenorganisationen der SPS, FDP und CVP (1971 bis 1995)*, Zürich: Chronos 2017.

of a mother living in Cameroon and a Swiss father. After being adopted, she came to Switzerland at the age of five. Tilo Frey was the first and last Black woman to be elected to the Swiss national parliament. In an interview in 2007, she recalled that before and after her election she was repeatedly described as a dirty N*, as Jovita dos Santos Pinto has pointed out.[25] During Tilo Frey's term of office, which lasted until 1975, she advocated for equal pay, the right to abortion and development cooperation. In addition, she worked as a teacher and later as a school director. In 2018, it was decided to rename Espace Louis Agassiz—a street on which the University of Neuchâtel's Faculty of Arts and Human Sciences is located—Espace Tilo Frey, to mark the ten-year anniversary since her death.

WOMEN'S RIGHT TO VOTE IN CULTURAL MEMORY

It was only in 2017 that the first feature film on the introduction of women's voting rights in Switzerland was made. The screenwriter and director, Petra Biondina Volpe, is both Italian and Swiss. In the same year, Mohamed Wa Baile published a children's book on this topic (the first to my knowledge).[26] Both authors have experienced migration. The main initiator behind the book on the lives of women in Appenzell was Renate Bräuniger. She was born in Germany and came to Switzerland to study sociology, where she married and remained. As editor and co-author, Bräuniger published 'FrauenLeben Appenzell', a book of 735 pages. Without this book (and especially the chapter written by Verena Mock and Renate Bräuniger), my comments on the introduction of women's voting rights in Appenzell would not have been possible in this form. According to Verena Mock, her article about Paky-Sutter would not have been written without this book project: 'I wouldn't know who else could have given me this assignment. I was not a historian either, but studied philosophy and German. As I come from a completely non-academic farming family, I had no network'.[27] Mock explained

---

[25] Jovita Dos Santos Pinto, Spuren. Eine Geschichte Schwarzer Frauen in der Schweiz, in Berlowitz, Joris, and Meierhofer-Mangeli, *Terra incognita? Der Treffpunkt Schwarzer Frauen in Zürich*, Zürich: Limmat Verlag 2013, 143–185, 160.

[26] Mohamed Wa Baile and Manuela Solinger, *Wie die Frauen zu ihren Rechten kamen*, Küsnacht: C. F. Portmann Verlag 2017.

[27] Statement made in a personal conversation, 29 April 2018 and via e-mail, 2 May 2018.

that her contribution went back to her 'Swiss Youth Research' work in 1988.[28] Although it was graded 'outstanding', the local publisher of the newspaper 'Appenzeller Volksfreund' did not want to include the work in its publication series 'Innerrhoder Schriften'. On the other hand, they had published the work of a classmate who had participated in the competition a year earlier, although it was much more subject specific and less readable (on the topic of the grammar of verbs in the Appenzell dialect). This offended her, but she never thought of making her own publication or looking for another publisher. No one would have asked her to make anything of it, until Renate Bräuniger came.

Julia Nentwich, whose interviews with women's voting rights activists were also extremely important for this chapter, obtained her doctorate at the University of Tübingen. She is now Professor of Psychology at the School of Humanities and Social Sciences of the University of St. Gallen. Regina Wecker, too, whom I quote several times in this study and who was the first female assistant at the History Department at the University of Basel and the first person in Switzerland to hold a chair for the history of women and gender (since 1997),[29] also came to Switzerland from Germany.[30] And the fact that the University of Zurich recently honoured Nadeschda Suslowa as a pioneer in the fight for women's access to universities is due to a suggestion by Professor Nada Boškovska.[31] Boškovska was born in Macedonia, but has lived in Switzerland since she was 9 years old.[32]

These examples show that it could be a stimulating undertaking to systematically investigate how, in Switzerland, women with experience of migration played a formative role in the establishment of women's and gender history (and more general gender studies).

---

[28] Verena Mock, *Das Frauenstimmrecht in Appenzell Innerrhoden. Geschichte einer verzögerten politischen Emanzipation*, Unpublished 1988.

[29] Ulla Bock, *Pionierarbeit. Die ersten Professorinnen für Frauen- und Geschlechterforschung an deutschsprachigen Hochschulen 1984–2014*, Frankfurt am Main: Campus 2015, 60.

[30] Francesca Falk and Peppina Beeli, Regina Wecker im Gespräch, *Bulletin der Schweizerischen Gesellschaft für Geschichte* 94 (2014), 20–23.

[31] https://www.hist.uzh.ch/de/ueberuns/forschungsmedien/20170410_boskovska1.html (12 December 2017).

[32] https://www.srf.ch/sendungen/musik-fuer-einen-gast/nada-boskovska-professorin-fuer-osteuropaeische-geschichte (12 June 2017).

Unseen Democratic Deficits in the Supposed Heartland of Democracy

Such an interrelation between migration and sociopolitical innovation can be observed not only in the case of female suffrage. Some years ago, a debate on how decisively the labour movement in Switzerland was influenced by people with experience of migration was conducted.[33] We can learn from this discussion to keep in mind the ambivalent situation that, on the one hand, 'foreigners' were often seen as strike-breakers and therefore an obstacle to the labour movement, and that, on the other hand, social movements were frequently labelled as coming from abroad, a strategy used in order to delegitimise them. In fact, even though different groups of 'migrants' made important contributions to the Swiss labour movement, it would be wrong to see them as being controlled from abroad and not only because these persons often became politicised in Switzerland itself. What is very interesting in such constellations are the relationships built up between the local population and the newcomers, as well as their ability to create novel alliances and to develop new ideas. There are still significant research gaps in this regard, even if there exists, for instance, some research analysing the impact of political refugees on the democratisation of Switzerland.[34]

However, such a perspective has so far rarely been applied systematically. Rather, the development of democracy is seen as a purely internal matter in Switzerland. In addition, the dominant picture of history depicts Switzerland as a heartland of democracy. Yet, if female suffrage is on

---

[33] Marc Vuilleumier, Quelques jalons pour une historiographie du mouvement ouvrier en Suisse, *Revue européenne des sciences sociales* XI, 29 (1973), 5–35. Charles Heimberg, La question de l'immigration, in Vallotton and Studer, *Histoire sociale et mouvement ouvrier, 1848–1998. Sozialgeschichte und Arbeiterbewegung, 1848–1998*, Lausanne: Editions d'en bas 1997, 155–161. Mattia Pelli, 'On n'avait peur de rien.' Immigrés et grève à la Monteforno de Bodio (1970–1972), *Cahiers d'histoire du mouvement ouvrier* 28, 93–114. Not only historians, but also social scientists studied such questions, see, for example, Mark James Miller, *Foreign Workers in Western Europe. An Emerging Political Force*, New York: Praeger 1981.

[34] See, for example, Werner G. Zimmermann, Asyl in der Schweiz. Aspekte und Dimensionen eines Dauerthemas, in Bankowski, Brang, Goehrke, and Zimmermann, *Asyl und Aufenthalt. Die Schweiz als Zuflucht und Wirkungsstätte von Slaven im 19. und 20. Jahrhundert*, Basel and Frankurt am Main: Helbling Lichtenhand 1994, 13–18. Ralf Prescher, Der Beitrag deutscher Immigranten zur Demokratieentwicklung in der Schweiz, in Roca, *Wege zur direkten Demokratie in den schweizerischen Kantonen. Schriften zur Demokratieforschung*, Zürich: Schulthess 2011, 175–201.

the radar, another picture appears. But in the light of the above-mentioned view of history, such democratic deficits simply become invisible.

'A NEW SWISS EXPORT ARTICLE: INSTRUCTION IN DEMOCRACY'

This can be shown, for instance, in a report published in a Swiss magazine in 1958.[35] Under the title 'A new Swiss export article: teaching in democracy', it is reported that—in the context of the imminent independence—an aid organisation (the later NGO Helvetas) had invited twelve Nigerian students to Switzerland to teach them about democracy.[36] The article defined Switzerland as a 'School of Democracy'. Its reporting focused, *nota bene*, mainly on a visit to a centre for basic military training and the Zurich city police—that is obviously where 'democracy' can be learned.

The fact that, in 1958, political participation was still denied to Swiss women at the national level was not mentioned in the article. Riehen was in fact the first municipality to introduce women's voting rights in 1958, and the first Swiss canton introduced women's suffrage in 1959. On the national level, in 1959 women's right to vote was rejected by a two-thirds majority. The fact that women in the south of Nigeria were given political rights earlier (in particular the year 1958 is seen as the official date of female enfranchisement in Southern Nigeria) is not mentioned in the article.

This, in turn, is hardly surprising, because if we were to look at the lack of women's voting rights, then Switzerland could no longer be understood to be the model of democracy. And the idea that perhaps the invited Nigerians could teach 'democracy' to Switzerland was obviously unthinkable.[37] The following statement from a discussion in the Swiss parliament about the introduction of female suffrage also reflects such a position.

[35] G. H., Ein neuer Schweizer Exportartikel: Unterricht in Demokratie, *Die Woche. Neue Schweizerische Illustrierte Zeitung, Die Woche. Neue Schweizerische Illustrierte Zeitung* 4. 10 August 1958 (1958), 4–5. I would cordially like to thank Elisabeth Joris for this indication.

[36] See also Dos Santos Pinto, Spuren. Eine Geschichte Schwarzer Frauen in der Schweiz, in Berlowitz, Joris, and Meierhofer-Mangeli, *Terra incognita? Der Treffpunkt Schwarzer Frauen in Zürich*, Zürich: Limmat Verlag 2013, 143–185, 156.

[37] With regard to the current media stereotyping of Nigerians in Switzerland and the long-term impact of colonialism on today's handling of migration, see Francesca Falk, Eine postkoloniale Perspektive auf die illegalisierte Immigration in der Schweiz. Über Ausschaffungen, den 'Austausch mit Afrika', Alltagsrassismus und die Angst vor der umgekehrten Kolonisierung, in Purtschert, Lüthi, and Falk, *Postkoloniale Schweiz. Formen und Folgen eines Kolonialismus ohne Kolonien*, Bielefeld: Transcript 2012, 201–224. A

In 1958, the National Council debated the vote to be held one year later. The Liberal member of parliament Jacques Chamorel supported holding a national vote for the following reasons: 'Where women's suffrage will have won an impressive majority, it must be introduced in the municipality or the canton; and in regions where it meets with strong opposition, at least proof will be given that there, in any case, it does not respond to a desire or a necessity'.[38] According to Yvonne Voegeli, he was probably one of those who agreed to the bill in the Council in order to reject it in the popular vote for men.[39] In this context, two others statements made by Chamorel in his speech are particularly noteworthy: 'It is not acceptable that the day after she married a Confederate, a foreigner who has never lived with us could immediately exercise the right to vote'. Chamorel therefore supported a vote about the introduction of female suffrage, but not female suffrage per se. In fact, it seemed particularly dangerous to him that those 'foreign' women who became Swiss by marriage should be able to vote immediately. Here, migration is thus used as an argument against women's voting rights.[40] Chamorel was full of praise for Switzerland's political system. He found that the existence of women's voting rights per se did not mean much: 'A *république nègre* can institute female suffrage, but it will nonetheless remain a *république nègre*, while Switzerland has multiplied the signs and evidence of its political maturity, even though women do not vote there'. From such a perspective, it is simply impossible for an African country to be more democratic than Switzerland, because whether it has women's suffrage or not—it remains a '*république nègre*'. Switzerland, on the other hand, cannot be undemocratic, no matter what the specific conditions are.

slightly modified re-publication of the article can be found online at Francesca Falk, Eine postkoloniale Perspektive auf die illegalisierte Immigration in der Schweiz. Über Ausschaffungen, den "Austausch mit Afrika", Alltagsrassismus und die Angst vor der umgekehrten Kolonisierung (2012), in: http://iae-journal.zhdk.ch/files/2012/12/AER6_Falk2.pdf (22 January 2013).

[38] Vormittagssitzung vom 20. März 1958. Séance du 20 mars 1958, matin. 7338. Frauenstimmrecht. Einführung Suffrage feminin. Introduction (1958), in: https://www.amtsdruckschriften.bar.admin.ch/viewOrigDoc/20036530.pdf?ID=20036530 (13 June 2018). My Translation.

[39] Voegeli, *Zwischen Hausrat und Rathaus. Auseinandersetzungen um die politische Gleichberechtigung der Frauen in der Schweiz 1945–1971*, Zürich: Chronos Verlag 1997, 255.

[40] This was also the case with regard to the argument that only women who moved to Switzerland wanted voting rights for women.

1929: FIGHTING WOMEN IN NIGERIA AND SWITZERLAND

In this respect, two incidents in Swiss and Nigerian history are highly interesting. In 1929, a petition was launched in Switzerland by the Swiss women's voting rights association.[41] In February, a nationwide appeal was published in the press, and in March, the collection of signatures began, which lasted 12 weeks. In the Bernese Oberland, the collection had to be stopped after the collectors had been insulted countless times. Nevertheless, within a short period of time, almost a quarter of a million signatures were gathered—a number never before reached in Switzerland.

In the same year, the Women's War took place in Nigeria. The rebellion, in which tens of thousands Eastern Nigerian women were involved, lasted about a month and extended over an area of six thousand square miles. British officials attributed the Women's War to the rumours that women were to be subjected to taxation. These rumours were used to mobilise women to oppose British rule.[42] An important element in the background to these protests was, however, also the fact that the colonial government had changed the position of women in society. Even if the position of women was not equal to that of men, Igbo women traditionally had important rights in the public domain and participated in policy-making.[43] When the British tried to create political institutions which monopolised power, they failed to acknowledge the political roles of women. Socialised in Victorian England, the colonisers discounted political institutions for women while they took into account the political institutions dominated by men. The women's traditional base of political power lay in assemblies of all of the adult women residing in a village. Here, they would discuss their particular interests as traders, farmers, wives, and mothers. These were often opposed to those of the men, and only collectively could they hold their own. If the women's requests were ignored, they would handle the matter by launching a boycott or a

[41] Hardmeier, *Frühe Frauenstimmrechtsbewegung in der Schweiz (1890–1930). Argumente, Strategien, Netzwerk und Gegenbewegung*, Zürich: Chronos Verlag 1997, 299–305.

[42] Toyin Falola and Adam Paddock, *The Women's War of 1929. A History of Anti-Colonial Resistance in Eastern Nigeria*, Durham, NC: Carolina Academic Press 2011, 97.

[43] In what follows, see Judith Van Allen, 'Sitting on a Man': Colonialism and the Lost Political Institutions of Igbo Women, *Canadian Journal of African Studies/Revue Canadienne des Études Africaines* 6, 2 (1972), 165–181.

strike or by 'sitting on a man'. In this case, women would gather at the residence of the offender. By invading his space, they forced him to pay attention. They danced and sang songs which specified their grievances against him and often called his manhood into question. Sometimes, they demolished his hut or plastered it with mud. This kind of protest was considered as legitimate by the local population. The Women's War practised 'sitting on a man' on a larger scale. The women 'sat on' numerous local chiefs to demand their resignation, damaged native courthouses, looted European trading firms, and blocked roads. The colonial troops fired on the protesters; more than fifty women were killed.

In Judith Van Allen view, despite some political changes initiated by the Women's War—the colonial authorities were forced, for instance, to replace some local rulers—women were thereafter excluded from most political processes in the colonial system.[44] She therefore regarded the Women's War as, ultimately, a failure. According to Van Allen, Western notions about gender roles imposed by the colonial regime blocked future large-scale political participation by women. As the political participation of women depended on the diffuseness of the political power, institutions on the Western model created a system in which there was 'no place for group solidarity, no place for what thereby became 'extra-legal' or simply illegal forms of group coercion, and thus very little place for women'.[45] In this way, the colonial state eliminated the women's ability to protect their own interests and made them dependent upon men for protection against other men.

Such a view has been contested by arguing that women continued to participate in Nigeria's political life. Researchers pointed out that the Women's War established a model for future protest. In addition, it changed the identity of its participants: women across southeastern Nigeria would transcend both the limits of their particular village and colonial administrative divisions by involving themselves in a mass

---

[44] Falola and Paddock, *The Women's War of 1929. A History of Anti-Colonial Resistance in Eastern Nigeria*, Durham, NC: Carolina Academic Press 2011, 99.

[45] Van Allen, 'Sitting on a Man': Colonialism and the Lost Political Institutions of Igbo Women, *Canadian Journal of African Studies/Revue Canadienne des Études Africaines* 6, 2 (1972), 165–181, 178.

movement. As a further result, these women were more closely studied that in any other area of Africa. From such a perspective, the Women's War is a historic example of both a feminist and an anti-colonial protest.

In Switzerland in 1929, the petition for female suffrage was delivered—after a small demonstration—to the *Bundeshaus*, the seat of the Swiss government and parliament. The petition, however, had no consequences. When it had been launched, the women's voting rights association deliberately refrained from initiating a popular initiative. The collection of signatures was intended to exert moral, but not direct political pressure. And so, shortly afterwards, a proposal was dropped to submit the petition—which had been signed by 170,000 women and 79,000 men—as a popular initiative. The collection of signatures was therefore used as an instrument of articulation, but not as a direct means of exerting pressure, because the Swiss women's voting rights association did not want to risk defeat in a vote.[46] As already mentioned, it was not until 1959 that the first national vote on women's voting rights took place in Switzerland (rejected by a two-thirds majority) and only in 1990 did the last Swiss canton introduce female suffrage.

---

[46] Sibylle Hardmeier, Neue Mobilisierungsstrategien und die Petition von 1929, in SVF, *Der Kampf um gleiche Rechte*, Basel: Schwabe Verlag 2009, 123–133, 131.

Open Access This chapter is licensed under the terms of the Creative Commons Attribution-NonCommercial-NoDerivatives 4.0 International License (http://creativecommons.org/licenses/by-nc-nd/4.0/), which permits any noncommercial use, sharing, distribution and reproduction in any medium or format, as long as you give appropriate credit to the original author(s) and the source, provide a link to the Creative Commons license and indicate if you modified the licensed material. You do not have permission under this license to share adapted material derived from this chapter or parts of it.

The images or other third party material in this chapter are included in the chapter's Creative Commons license, unless indicated otherwise in a credit line to the material. If material is not included in the chapter's Creative Commons license and your intended use is not permitted by statutory regulation or exceeds the permitted use, you will need to obtain permission directly from the copyright holder.

CHAPTER 7

Conclusion: An Awareness of Alternatives

Abstract My findings show that contemporary and historiographical discourses which predominantly frame migration as a problem to be tackled, neglect the historical evidence for sociopolitical innovation that can, at times, result from international, transnational, internal, and even indirect experiences of migration. For instance, this book gives various examples that show how the existence of privilege and discrimination can generate social change. To illuminate such links between migration and gender innovation does not mean glorifying migration or propagating a naïve notion of diversity. Migration is per se neither good nor bad, but the conditions under which it takes place are good or bad, and these conditions are made, not given. The political, economic, and social conditions under which migration takes place depend on how past and present migration is perceived. This is precisely why, today, we have to make visible these often hidden histories. Looking at history through the lens of migration not only adds new insights to an established body of work, but changes the perspective under which our past and thus also our present is told—and our future imagined.

Keywords Anti-Muslim racism · The fear of 'Italianisation' · Limitations of this study · Past · Present · Future

Equal Rights Presented as Being Endangered by Migration

Equal rights are often presented as being endangered by migration. For example, in the case of Switzerland, a constitutional ban on minarets has been legitimised by a prominent feminist with reference to women's rights.[1] In academia, two prominent political scientists have claimed that the 'true clash of civilisations' would concern 'gender equality and sexual liberalisation'.[2] Today, when gender equality is perceived as being endangered by migration, suspicion is primarily focused on Muslim 'migrants'. However, in the boom years after the Second World War, this was not a prominent issue in Switzerland. In the public debates of the 1960s, the religious affiliation of workers from Turkey and certain territories of former Yugoslavia in fact played a minor role.[3]

Interestingly, in those years, Italians[4] were often presented in a similar way to Muslims today. Of course, this does not imply that there

---

[1] However, Julia Onken's argumentation was criticised by different women's groups, see for example http://www.inforel.ch/fileadmin/user_upload/dateien/OffenerBriefJuliaOnken.pdf (23 June 2016) as well as Elisabeth Joris and Katrin Rieder, Not in our name, in Gross, Krebs, Schaffner, and Stohler, *Von der Provokation zum Irrtum. Menschenrechte und Demokratie nach dem Minarett-Bauverbot*, St-Ursanne: Editions le Doubs 2010, 25–36. In this context, see also Stefanie C. Boulila, Insignificant Signification: A Feminist Critique of the Anti-Muslim Feminist, in Hafez, *Jahrbuch für Islamophobieforschung*, Wien: New Academic Press 2013, 88–103. Carolin Fischer and Janine Dahinden, *Changing Gender Representations in Politics of Belonging: A Critical Analysis of Developments in Switzerland* (2016), http://nccr-onthemove.ch/publications/changing-gender-representations-in-politics-of-belonging-a-critical-analysis-of-developments-in-switzerland (1 December 2016).

[2] Ronald Inglehart and Pippa Norris, The True Clash of Civilizations, *Foreign Policy* (2003), 62–70, 64–65. For a critique of this position, see Éric Fassin, National Identities and Transnational Intimacies: Sexual Democracy and the Politics of Immigration in Europe, *Public Culture. An Interdisciplinary Journal of Transnational Cultural Studies* 22, 3 (2010), 507–529.

[3] Giuseppe De Simone, Von Türken und Kurden zu Muslimen? Eine Untersuchung der Berichterstattung in den Schweizer Printmedien über die Einwanderer aus der Türkei, 1960-2006, in Ideli, Suter Reich, and Kieser, *Neue Menschenlandschaften. Migration Türkei - Schweiz 1961–2011*, Zürich: Chronos 2011, 141–158; Samuel-Martin Behloul, Muslime als die neuen 'Anderen'. 9/11 und die Folgen, in *Tangram* 6 (2013), 70–73; Thomas Bürgisser, Wahrnehmungswandel der jugoslawischen Migrationsbevölkerung, *Tangram* 6 (2013), 42–46; Patrik Ettinger, Muslime in den Medien zunehmend problematisiert, *Tangram* 12 (2017), 69–74.

[4] This applies to other groups as well. In general, people from the 'south' and later on from ex-Yugoslavia were perceived in this way.

are no differences between the past depiction of Italian migration and the current representation of Muslim migration to Switzerland. For instance, even though Italians were seen as causing a religious imbalance in Switzerland, the image of the Italians was not reduced to religion and in fact oscillated between Italians as associated with either conservatism or communism. In addition, Italians were never linked as closely to the topic of terrorism as Muslims are today, even though 'Italian Communists working in Switzerland [...] were seen as a potential security threat'.[5] Furthermore, since Italians were perceived as being more fertile than the Swiss, it was feared that an 'Italianisation' of the Swiss population could not be prevented.[6] Likewise—and somewhat ironically, in a country where many prided themselves on owning a Swiss army knife and where men kept their military rifles at home—Italians men were perceived as dangerous because they were allegedly wont to carry switchblades.[7] Other customs that met with disapproval were the black mourning clothes worn by some Italian widows and the fact that, in church, certain Italian women wore a veil.[8] Moreover, 'migrants' liked to use railway stations as meeting points,[9] and such gatherings were viewed critically, in part because Italians were considered more likely to sexually harass Swiss women.[10] For example, in 1983, a snack bar in the

---

[5] Mark James Miller, *Foreign Workers in Western Europe. An Emerging Political Force*, New York: Praeger 1981, 5.

[6] E.H., Briefe an die NZZ. Italianisierung der Schweiz?, in Neue Zürcher Zeitung, 11 September 1964 (Mittagsausgabe) (1964), 59. See also Damir Skenderovic, Die Macht rechtspopulistischer Aussenseiter in den 1960er bis 1980er Jahren, in Skenderovic and D'Amato, *Mit dem Fremden politisieren. Rechtspopulistische Parteien und Migrationspolitik in der Schweiz seit den 1960er Jahren*, Zürich: Chronos 2008, 31–67, 42.

[7] Thomas Buomberger, *Kampf gegen unerwünschte Fremde. Von James Schwarzenbach bis Christoph Blocher*, Zürich: Orell Füssli 2004, 81.

[8] Marc Virot, *Vom Anderssein zur Assimilation. Merkmale zur Beurteilung der Assimilationsreife der Ausländer in der Schweiz*, Bern: Haupt 1968, 59.

[9] This was also the case in Germany: Sabine Hess, Politiken der (Un-)Sichtbarmachung. Eine Kritik der Wissens- und Bilderproduktion zu Migration, in Yildiz and Hill, *Nach der Migration. Postmigrantische Perspektiven jenseits der Parallelgesellschaft*, Bielefeld: Transcript 2015, 49–64, 50.

[10] Angelo Maiolino, Die 'Tschinggen' und die Schwarzenbach-Initiative. Von der Politik der Marginalisierten zur Mediterranisierung der Schweiz (2012), http://www.terra-cognita.ch/fileadmin/user_upload/terracognita/documents/terra_cognita_21.pdf (15 June 2016). Angelo Maiolino, *Als die Italiener noch Tschinggen waren. Der Widerstand gegen die Schwarzenbach-Initiative*, Zürich: Rotpunktverlag 2011.

town of Will refused to seat Italians towards the front of the premises, claiming that unaccompanied women would no longer dare to enter.[11] In addition, regardless of Swiss society's own shortcomings regarding gender equality, Italian families were often characterised as patriarchal. Remarkably, the topic of the 'isolated foreign wife' can also be found in these years. In a report published in 1976 by the 'Federal Advisory Commission for the Foreigner Problem', it was acknowledged, for instance, that the employment rate among married foreign women was relatively high. Nonetheless, the report stated that wives coming from southern regions lived more narrowly within the family circle than Swiss women, having little opportunity for contact with the outside world.[12] The stereotypical images of the 'oppressed and isolated Muslima' and the 'patriarchal Muslim' thus possess some traits that, from a historical perspective, are quite familiar. Such a characterisation recalls once again the strategies of legitimisation associated with colonialism, condensed in Gayatri Spivak's words that 'White men are saving brown women from brown men'.[13] Given these recurring images, I believe it is crucial to engage in an in-depth historical analysis of situations where migration was a driving force for emancipatory change.

Migration and the Creation of New Ideas and Practices

In fact, the 'contribution of migration to the creation of new ideas (not just their spread) has been underemphasised in previous analyses'.[14] Patrick Manning sees especially cross-community migration as driving development. However, by characterising this form of migration as male,

---

[11] See the broadcast produced by DRS aktuell (Swiss Radio and Television), 23 December 1983.

[12] 'Im übrigen lebt die Ehefrau aus südlichen Regionen mehr als die Schweizerin im Familienkreis. Sie hat wenige Kontaktmöglichkeiten mit der Aussenwelt, obschon die Erwerbsquote bei den verheirateten Ausländerinnen verhältnismässig hoch liegt'. Eidgenössische Konsultativkommission für das Ausländerproblem, *Menschliche Probleme der Arbeitskräfte und ihrer Familienangehörigen*, Bern: EKA 1976, 20.

[13] Gayatri Spivak, Can the Subaltern Speak?, in Grossberg and Nelson, *Marxism and the Interpretation of Culture*, Urbana: Chicago University of Illinois Press 1988, 271–316, 296.

[14] Patrick Manning, Cross-Community Migration: A Distinctive Human Pattern, *Social Evolution & History* 5, 2 (2006), 24–54, 46.

he marginalises females as historical agents, as Donna Gabaccia has rightly pointed out.[15] Moreover, '[m]oving from the countryside to the nearest town or city can be just as much an occasion of knowledge creation as the relocation from one continent to another', as Simone Lässig and Swen Steinberg have convincingly argued by, at the same time, highlighting how productive the intersection between the history of knowledge and the history of migration is.[16] It is therefore not a coincidence that people with some kind of migration experience have often developed a different view of history. In the field of migration research, too, scientific innovation often originated from people with migration experience.[17]

Once our attention has been drawn to such historical processes, important aspects of the past appear in a new light. For instance, when certain privileges intersect with specific forms of discrimination, the resulting situations offer the potential for new social and political configurations, as we have seen in relation to various examples. Likewise, the knowledge and motivation needed to push for change can circulate through various forms of migration and new networks and alliances of resistance can thereby be forged.[18] Moreover, those who happen to not comply with a norm because they are used to different standards of

---

[15] Donna R. Gabaccia, Gender and Migration, in Ness, *The Encyclopedia of Global Human Migration*, Malden: Wiley-Blackwell 2013, https://onlinelibrary.wiley.com/doi/book/10.1002/9781444351071 (3 Febraury 2014).

[16] Simone Lässig and Swen Steinberg, Knowledge on the Move: New Approaches Towards a History of Migrant Knowledge, *Geschichte und Gesellschaft* 43, 3 (2017), 313–346, 316.

[17] Helma Lutz and Kathy Davis, Biographische Grenzüberschreitungen und feministische Imagionation: Avtar Brah, Seyla Benhabib und Rosi Braidotti, in Lutz, *Gender mobil? Geschlecht und Migration in transnationalen Räumen*, Münster: Verlag Westfälisches Dampfboot 2009, 251–270; Kijan Espahangizi, Migrationsforschung und epistemische Teilhabe. Vier historische Schlaglichter auf die Zürcher 'Fremdarbeitersoziologie' in den 1970er Jahren, in Morawek and Krenn, *Urban Citizenship. Demokratisierung der Demokratie*, Wien: VfmK 2017, 89–111; Kijan Espahangizi, The Granddaughter's Dissertation: Some Thoughts on Knowledge about Migration in 1960s Switzerland (2017), https://historyofknowledge.net/2017/08/10/the-granddaughters-dissertation/ (4 June 2018).

[18] I analyse this topic in relation to deportations during Italian Fascism in Francesca Falk, Deportations, the Spreading of Dissent and the Development of Democracy. The confino on Ponza and Ventotene during Italian Fascism and its Political Aftermath, *Journal of Migration History*, forthcoming.

behaviour may even unintentionally call these very norms into question. In addition, since relationships of power are naturalised by their everyday presence, they can sometimes be more easily perceived by newcomers. Their gaze can defamiliarise the familiar[19] and in this way produce an 'awareness of alternatives', as Peter Burke has pointed out.[20]

As interviews with aging couples who migrated from Italy to Switzerland have shown, the experience of leaving a familiar environment and finding one's way in a new one—which often does not classify 'migrants' as belonging—can provide specific resources.[21] These can be helpful in later stages of life, which are also associated with the loss of familiar contexts and thereby producing constraints for reorientation. Experiences of migration thus prove to be a specific 'capital' for dealing with changes and uncertainties. This is all the more important because individuals with experiences of migration are often confronted with specific difficulties upon retirement, for example, with regard to their pension. However, if today the so-called guest workers can also be seen as pioneers of globalisation,[22] then the burden often associated with this experience of migration must not be forgotten. Nor should globalisation be glorified. Nevertheless, it is important to emphasise such resources, as they usually fall out of the picture.[23]

CHANGING THE PERSPECTIVE UNDER WHICH OUR PAST IS TOLD AND OUR FUTURE IMAGINED

The approach proposed here does not merely consist in adding new information to an established account, but, in fact, to change perspectives and thereby to challenge some fundamental assumptions.

---

[19] Lloyd S. Kramer, *Threshold of a New World. Intellectuals and the Exile Experience in Paris, 1830–1848*, Ithaca, London: Cornell University Press 1988, 2.

[20] Peter Burke, *Exiles and Expatriates in the History of Knowledge, 1500–2000*, Waltham, MA: Brandeis University Press 2017, 23.

[21] In what follows, see Eva Soom Ammann, *Ein Leben hier gemacht. Altern in der Migration aus biographischer Perspektive. Italienische Ehepaare in der Schweiz*, Bielefeld: Transcript 2011.

[22] Erol Yildiz, Einleitung, in Yildiz and Hill, *Nach der Migration. Postmigrantische Perspektiven jenseits der Parallelgesellschaft*, Bielefeld: Transcript 2015, 9–16, 11.

[23] With regard to the specific resources of the so-called second generation, see Rohit Jain, *Kosmopolitische Pioniere: 'Inder_innen der zweiten Generation' aus der Schweiz zwischen Assimilation, Exotik und globaler Moderne*, Bielefeld: Transcript 2018.

For instance, assertions have been made which become much more complicated if the living conditions of 'migrants' are taken into account. See, for instance, the statement that in these boom years, the opportunity to live on a single income made the employment of women optional. If we look at 'migrant' families, the limitations of this statement immediately catch our eye.

Whereas over the past decades, 'dozens of publications have thus appeared that started out by saying that the field of gender and migration is in general underresearched',[24] this observation no longer holds true today. Nevertheless, the literature is still lopsided, and many stimulating questions await a systematic investigation, as we have seen.

Of course, the examples I have analysed in this contribution are not intended to suggest that, for *all* possible phenomena related to changing gender relations, migration was *the* decisive factor. Sometimes, migration is only one factor among many (new ideas and role models can, for instance, circulate via the media). In addition, I am obviously aware that migration characterises our society in many different and sometimes ambiguous ways and that my investigation necessarily privileges the 'productive' aspects of it. My findings do not imply therefore that migration can never be an obstacle in the struggle for gender equality. In regard to highly skilled 'migrant' women in Switzerland, Yvonne Riaño has shown, for instance, that traditional ideas about gender roles, discourses about ethnic difference, and discriminatory migration policies intersect and hinder these women from accessing the upper segments of the Swiss labour market. For them, '[m]igration, therefore, does not always imply empowerment and emancipation, but also generates new forms of social inequality'.[25] Mirjana Morokvasic also crities a simplistic perception of emigration as empowerment.[26] Nor do I argue that we should allow only those migrations that benefit the receiving society. From my perspective,

---

[24] Marlou Schrover, Europe: Gender and Migration, in Ness, *The Encyclopedia of Global Human Migration*, Malden: Wyler 2013, https://onlinelibrary.wiley.com/doi/book/10.1002/9781444351071 (3 Febraury 2014).

[25] Yvonne Riaño, Drawing New Boundaries of Participation: Experiences and Strategies of Economic Citizenship among Skilled Migrant Women in Switzerland, *Environment and Planning* 43, 7 (2011), 1530–1546, 1530.

[26] Mirjana Morokvasic, Migration, Gender, Empowerment, in *Lutz, Gender mobil? Geschlecht und Migration in transnationalen Räumen*, Münster: Westfälisches Dampfboot 2009, 28–51; Mirjana Morokvasic, Gender, Labour, and Migration, in Ness, *The Encyclopedia of Global Human Migration*, Malden: Wiley 2013.

the legitimacy of migration does not depend on whether it is useful for any particular individual or group.[27] Finally, my focus on the complex links between migration and gender equality should not be equated with the promotion of a single, linear success story. Ambiguity, counter-movements, setbacks, and moments of failure are, as we know, always part of history.[28] And of course, the argument is not that all 'migrants' are politically progressive, which is obviously not the case. It is quite well-known that the experience of migration can sometimes also lead to an increased conservatism, also in regard to gender relations. Moreover, there are clear limitations to this study. For instance, in the examples analysed in this book, the existence of two genders is not questioned. This book has therefore a direction, but no end. Many other fields would be worthwhile to investigate.

What my findings do show, however, is that contemporary and historiographical discourses which predominantly frame migration as a problem to be tackled neglect the historical evidence for sociopolitical innovation that can, at times, result from international, transnational,

---

[27] The philosopher Andreas Cassee, for example, demands that every person should be free to decide in which country he or she wants to live. From such a perspective, restrictions on immigration are only permissible in exceptional situations. Andreas Cassee, *Globale Bewegungsfreiheit. Ein philosophisches Plädoyer für offene Grenzen*, Berlin: Suhrkamp 2016.

[28] I can give here three very different examples indicating such forms of ambiguity, counter-movements, and setbacks. For instance, it has been argued that the more legal hindrances women have broken through, the more heavily images of female beauty have come to weigh upon them. Naomi Wolf, *The Beauty Myth*, London: Chatto & Windus 1990.

Another example for a very concrete setback is the fact that since 2003, the proportion of women has been declining in the Swiss Council of States, https://www.parlament.ch/de/%C3%BCber-das-parlament/fakten-und-zahlen/zahlen-ratsmitglieder (27 April 2018).

Furthermore, feminist positions were integrated with ambivalent consequences into a neoliberal agenda. For instance, emancipatory demands were incorporated under very specific conditions, in a way that the flexibilisation of working hours, an important feminist demand of the new women's movement, led to the fact that employers now have more easily access to workers at home. Patricia Purtschert and Nina Apin, 'Ich ärgere mich den ganzen Tag! Dauernd!' (2017), http://www.taz.de/Archiv-Suche/!5397174&s=nina+apin&SuchRahmen=Print (1 June 2017).

internal, and even indirect experiences of migration.²⁹ It is only from a historical perspective that we can recognise how profoundly the social and political developments are shaped by migration.³⁰

To illuminate the link between migration and what I call gender innovation does not mean to glorify migration or to propagate a naïve notion of diversity.³¹ Migration is per se neither good nor bad, but the conditions under which it takes place are good or bad, and these conditions are made, not given. The political, economic, and social conditions under which migration takes place depend on how past and present migration is perceived. This is precisely why, today, we have to make visible these often hidden histories. Looking at history through the lens of migration not only adds some new insights to an established body of work, but changes the perspective under which our past and thus also our present is told—and our future imagined.

---

²⁹ Walter Leimgruber has repeatedly stressed the importance of such a perspective. Walter Leimgruber, Die Tücken der Entgrenzung. Migration und Migrationsforschung vor neuen Herausforderungen, in Picard, Chakkalakal, and Andris, *Grenzen aus kulturwissenschaftlichen Perspektiven*, Berlin: Panama Verlag 2016, 269–296; Walter Leimgruber, Demokratische Rechte auf Nicht-Staatsbürger ausweiten, in Abbt and Rochel, *Migrationsland Schweiz. 15 Vorschläge für die Zukunft*, Baden: Hier und Jetzt 2016, 21–37.

³⁰ In this context, a highly interesting institute is the newly founded INES: https://institutneueschweiz.ch (12 September 2017).

³¹ For a critical perspective on migration perceived as either a problem or as potential see Kijan Espahangizi, Im Wartesaal der Integration, in: terra cognita. *Potenzial. Potentiel. Potenziale* 27 (2015), 104–108; Rohit Jain, 'Sprichst Du Hindi?'—die zweite Generation zwischen Potenzial und Problem, *terra cognita. Potenzial. Potentiel. Potenziale* 27 (2015), 94–97; Rohit Jain and Shalini Randeria, Wider den Migrationskomplex—Perspektiven auf eine andere Schweiz, in *Sozialalmanach. Herein: Alle(s) für die Zuwanderung* (2015), 199–210.

Open Access This chapter is licensed under the terms of the Creative Commons Attribution-NonCommercial-NoDerivatives 4.0 International License (http://creativecommons.org/licenses/by-nc-nd/4.0/), which permits any noncommercial use, sharing, distribution and reproduction in any medium or format, as long as you give appropriate credit to the original author(s) and the source, provide a link to the Creative Commons license and indicate if you modified the licensed material. You do not have permission under this license to share adapted material derived from this chapter or parts of it.

The images or other third party material in this chapter are included in the chapter's Creative Commons license, unless indicated otherwise in a credit line to the material. If material is not included in the chapter's Creative Commons license and your intended use is not permitted by statutory regulation or exceeds the permitted use, you will need to obtain permission directly from the copyright holder.

The manufacturer's authorised representative in the EU is Springer Nature Customer Service Centre GmbH, Europaplatz 3, 69115 Heidelberg, Germany. If you have any concerns regarding our products, please contact ProductSafety@springernature.com

Printed and bound by CPI Group (UK) Ltd, Croydon, CR0 4YY
23/03/2026
02076402-0001